THE WISDOM OF FAITH

• • • • •

Essays in Honor of
Dr. Sebastian Alexander Matczak

• • • • •

Henry O. Thompson
Editor

UNIVERSITY
PRESS OF
AMERICA

Lanham • New York • London

Copyright © 1989 by

University Press of America,® Inc.

4720 Boston Way
Lanham, MD 20706

3 Henrietta Street
London WC2E 8LU England

British Cataloging in Publication Information Available

Library of Congress Cataloging-in-Publication Data

The Wisdom of faith : essays in honor of Dr. Sebastian Alexander Matczak /
Henry O. Thompson, editor.
p.   cm.
Includes bibliographies.
1. Religion—Philosophy. 2. Religions.   3. Philosophy.   4. Matczak, Sebastian A.
I. Matczak, Sebastian A.   II. Thompson, Henry O.
BL51.W64   1989   200'.1—dc20   89–31915 CIP

ISBN 0–8191–7436–X (alk. paper)

TABLE OF CONTENTS

SEBASTIAN ALEXANDER MATCZAK

PRE-WORD

The preface, "the word that comes before," is an opportunity for acknowledgements and disclaimers. The latter is the easier of the two. The authors of these essays speak for themselves. They have written in academic freedom from their own perspective.

The former is the greater challenge but challenges are more fun. Someone once asked why I worked so hard. I said the truth is that I'm hardly working. Partly that is acknowledgement of my own inefficiency which often seems more like mere fiddling than work. But part of it also is that it has been my privilege, rather rare I find in the world at large, to be able to spend much of my time doing things that I want to do and enjoy doing. A colleague once chortled that he was having the time of his life - having fun and making money. I may not make much money but I can appreciate the forepart of his statement.

A part of that enjoyment is honoring a scholar in his later years after considerable achievement with the hope that he will live many more and add yet other accomplishments to his "stable" as publishers say in the book trade. A part of the joy is the opportunity to say "Thank you" to all who have made this work possible. I appreciate the support for this effort given by Therese Stewart and Joyce E. Thompson. Joyce has not only sketched several drawings but prepared the index as well. Anyone who has done the latter, knows the monumental effort involved while those who use indexes know their value.

There is joy in the thankful recognition of the authors of these essays whose work here appears in print. They have gone through hard labor and given birth to their brain children and we can rejoice in the morning that a child a born, a child is given, to paraphrase a biblical phrase. The labor brings to

v

birth but even in that precious time of delivery there is the awareness of a givenness to work, to labor, to this ephemeral thing called scholarship.

An administrator said she did not understand publishing; no sense in it. Another, more to my liking, admitted her inability to do this herself but appreciated the life giving dynamic of the mind giving birth. While she did not work with the Word herself, she could facilitate the work of those who did. That too brought joy in the morning (Psalm 30:5) not to mention throughout the heat of the day (Matthew 20:12). One should note administrators who administer <u>and</u> who publish, both. And scholarship is not limited to publication but appears in the classroom and the board room, in the highways and byways of life even as does the wisdom which is the theme of the following pages.

The "pre-word" is in a word, simply a chance to say thank you to all who have made this volume possible, including the one who inspired its conception.

Henry O. Thompson

A LEADING INWARD

The Wisdom of Faith extends to all of life. Some people associate faith with religion, and perhaps rightly so. But then they truncate it with a merely traditional religion. All of life is religion or in Paul Tillich's words, everyone has an ultimate concern. Or from the perspective of the truncators, there are the facts as with scientific fact and then when we go beyond the facts, we go by faith. The truth, of course, is that scientific fact is scientific faith. Real scientists are well aware that we deal with probabilities which the common man and the unscrupulous call facts. Or to put it another way, faith is a fact of life. Or shall we say the probability of life? One must hasten to add that it is not only science which is a religion but politics, athletics, computer programming and other human activities not usually associated with faith.[1]

The atheist often reminds theists that you cannot prove the existence of God while they ignorantly or dishonestly ignore the alternative. Neither can you disprove the existence of God. And of course the same goes for all other aspects of life, including the agnostic position at the vortex of the dichotomy that one cannot prove nor disprove anything, including this sentence. And yet in ordinary life as well as extraordinary, we do manage to go on living - by faith. That faith may be in the elemental physicality of life - eat, drink and be merry. It may be in a capitalistic ideology or some new messiah.[2] It may be in the scientific method or the Almighty Dollar. Some people even believe in God, a very present help in time of trouble (Ps 46:1b). But the agnostic fact remains that we do continue.

A long time ago, Ecclesiastes or Qoheleth, the Preacher, observed that all is vanity - mist, vapor, foolish pride - with the appearance of reality but without its substance (1:2). Death comes to the wise as well as the fool (2:16). Still, the "bottom line" is that wisdom has a practical value in relating to reality (7:12, 9:13-18).

That reality includes the iconoclastic treatment of conventions and a faith in information and openness as Lars Aagaard-Mogensen discusses here the issues of freedom, religion and socio-logic. It includes the faith of nationalism which Walter S. Harris points out bids fair to being the real faith that binds the hearts of earth's sundry tribes. A much older faithful wisdom is that of the mystics but Walter Houston Clark sketches some new wrinkles in the old tradition in the growing number of reports of Near Death Experiences (NDE). We can guess that mysticism is as old as humanity, judging perhaps by the fetal position of Neanderthal burials with red ochre sprinkled on them. One interpretation is that people expected the dead to have a rebirth and the ochre was the blood of a new life. Speculation lessens with the written word and the beginning of history but even here there are problems of interpretation.

From the earliest days of writing, we catch glimpses and then whole writings of the wisdom tradition in the ancient Near East, the ancient Egyptian, Indian and Chinese traditions. In some ways, the biblical record is a distillation of that larger horizon which is with us still. It continues in the serviceman's New Testament with Psalms and Proverbs and it continues in traditional faith as Theodore James points out in his philosophical theology. It continues in Tsirpanlis' efforts to unravel the tangled skein of Byzantine politics which in the 17th century allied Eastern Orthodox and Reformers against Roman Catholicism. That has left a legacy of confusion leaving us to wonder about the wisdom of ecumenical politics mixed with ethnic policies. The wisdom tradition also continues in Confucianism, Islam and Buddhism as exemplified here in the work of Philip Hwang, Y.M. Ozturk and The Venerable Sunanda Putuwar.

Of these last three, Confucius represents the practical this world approach "par excellence." Here we have some common ground with the wisdom tradition of the ancient Near East. Putuwar's view of Buddhism may surprise a few whose stereotype of that faith is as far removed from the practical as the East is from the West. Islam's Sufism relates to the earlier concern with the mystical but it eventuates in a return to the practicalities of life.

And this continues in the mythic tradition both as related to and distinct from the mystical. Roger W. Wescott notes the continuing theme of creation, fall, redemption and restoration. In one form or another, we find it, or elements of it in many traditions. It has resurfaced in recent decades in the so-called "new religions." The myth of the eternal return[3] recurs in faith and hope though wisdom tells us it - or predictions of it - has happened many times before. Still the faith persists that maybe the time is at hand when the new age will dawn and all the earth will be paradise.[4] If this is the time, wisdom may help us recognize it and guide us in making the most of it. In the meanwhile, we settle for Reinhold Niebuhr and his "serenity prayer."

O God, give us serenity to accept what cannot be changed, courage to change what should be changed, and wisdom to distinguish the one from the other.[5]

FOOTNOTES

1. Thomas S. Kuhn, The Structure of Scientific Revolutions 2nd ed; Chicago: University of Chicago, 1970. Michael Polanyi, Personal Knowledge: Towards a Post-Critical Philosophy; Chicago: University of Chicago, 1962. Bruce Kuklick, The Good Ruler: From Herbert Hoover to Richard Nixon; New Brunswick and London: Rutgers University Press, 1988, notes that politics is less a business than a religion.

2. James Russell Lowell (1819-1891), "The Present Crisis," 1844. Stanza 5 has the words "some new messiah..."

3. Mircea Eliade, The Myth of the Eternal Return; Princeton: Princeton University, 1971 (original, 1954).

4. J. Addington Symonds (1840-1893), "The Days That Are to Be."

5. Reinhold Niebuhr (1892-1971), "Prayer," 1934.

SEBASTIAN ALEXANDER MATCZAK

It is the teachers art
to let us live with him

and what we take
he rarely knows;

A moment of astonishment
when beauty sets
his brain aflame:

A striking blow of truth
which shatters what is known
and is not so:

A startled cry of look
and then we see.

A teacher lives in what he is
In what we are to be.

Raymond John Baughan, 1965
The Sound of Silence[1]

It has been said that education is caught as much as it is taught. In the case of Dr. Sebastian Alexander Matczak, one should say it is both. The above bit of verse thus applies to his life and career as a teacher even as the focus here is his life as a scholar. Sir Sarvepelli Radhakrishnan, one of the greatest Indian philosophers who ever lived, said, "Philosophy as logical reflection is different from philosophy as the love of wisdom. 'Sophia' or wisdom is not mere knowledge. It is knowledge lived. It is a way of life where valid knowledge is the condition of just action."[2]

Dr. Matczak was born in Warsaw, Poland, 20 Jan 14,

to John or Jan (a builder) and Genowefa (Jagodzinska). We write this festschrift in celebration of his 75 years of teaching and scholarship.

Formally, the former includes Warsaw University (1946-1947), The Lycee in Paris (1952-1953) and Manhattan College in New York (1956-1957). He started teaching at St. Johns University on Long Island 1957. Here he became a full professor in 1965 and has continued as Adjunct Professor in the Graduate School since 1980. He started teaching at the Unification Theological Seminary 1975.

His scholarship is shown in his extensive education. He holds three master's degrees: Cracow Seminary or School of Philosophy (M.Ph., 1938), Warsaw University (Master's in History, 1942) and Warsaw School of Theology (M.Th., 1944). He holds three doctorates: Gregorian University in Rome (S.T.D. in Dogmatic Theology, 1951-2), Catholic Institute in Paris (Ph.D. in Philosophy, 1958), University of Paris, Sorbonne (Ph.D. in Philosophy, 1963).[3]

Dr. Matczak's educational background is reflected in his linguistic ability. He speaks and writes Polish, of course, but also German, French, Italian and English. Besides all that, he has a good knowledge of Latin and classical Greek.

His scholarship is reflected in his professional associations. He has been a member of the Academy of Science in New York (1983), the Academy of Religion and Health, the American Association of University Professors, the Association of American Philosophy, the Association of Catholic American Philosophy, the Fellowship of Religious Humanists, the International Social Science Honor Society (Delta Tau Kappa), The Polish Institute of Arts and Sciences in America, the Societa Tomista Internazionale (Rome), the Society of History of Science, The Society for the Scientific Study of Religion, and the Society of Theology in America.

Above all, Dr. Matczak's scholarly career appears in his many publications where he has made many contributions to his field of philosophy of religion where he has specialized in the history of philosophy, especially modern and contemporary metaphysics.

PUBLICATIONS

1938

Emmanuel Kant on Space and Time; Cracow: School of Philosophy (Master's Thesis in Philosophy).

1942

The Election of Jacob Swinka to the Archbishopric of Gniezno (Poland, XIII C.); Warsaw: University of Warsaw (Master's Thesis in History).

1944

Sources to the Biography of Peter Bembus (XVI C.); Warsaw: School of Theology (Master's Thesis in Theology).

1951

Stanislaus Cardinal Hosius on Sacraments in General; Rome: Pontificia Universitas Gregoriana (in Polish and Latin). (S.T.D. dissertation, "Stanislaus Hosius on Scaraments" (XVI C., Reformation). Cardinal Hosius lived from 1504-1579.

1952

Stanislaus Hosius on Sacraments; Paris: Libella (in Polish).

1958

Karl Barth on the Existence of God (Ph.D.

dissertation, "Karl Barth on the Existence of God," Catholic Institute of Paris, 1958).

1961

"Stanislaus Cardinal Hosius: Present State of Research - Results and Postulates," The Polish Review VI, No. 4 (Aut 61), 45-60. The Review is cited hereafter as PR.

1962

Karl Barth on God: Our Knowledge of the Divine Existence; NY, Rome, London, Paris: St. Paul Publishers (Alba House). 358 pp.

Reviewed by Robert F. Conway, PR VIII, No. 1 (Wint 63), 124- 125, who compared the work to that of Kung, von Balthasar, Hamer and Bouillard.

1963

Karl Barth (Ph.D. dissertation, University of Paris [Sorbonne]).

"An Archiepiscopal Election in the Middle Ages: Jacob II Swinka of Gniezo," PR VIII, No. 1 (Wint 63), 21-55. Swinka served from 1283-1314.

1964

"A Select and Classified Bibliography of David Hume," The Modern Schoolman XLII (Nov 64), 70-81.

1967

"Fideism," The New Catholic Encyclopedia II:278-280; NY: McGraw-Hill.

"Traditionalism," V:228-230; ibid.

1968

President of Learned Publications, Inc., New York

[Interdisciplinary Publications]. 83-53 Manton Street, Jamaica, NY. 1968 -.

Editor in Chief, Philosophical Questions Series [PQS]; Louvain: Nauwelaerts, 1968 - and NY: Learned Publications.

Le probleme de Dieu dans la pensee de Karl Barth [PQS, No. 1]. (Ph.D. dissertation, "Karl Barth," University of Paris, Sorbonne, 1963).

Research and Composition in Philosophy [PQS, No. 2].

1970

Philosophy: A Select, Classified Bibliography in Ethics, Economics, Law, Politics, Sociology [PQS, No. 3].

"Preface," Mary R. Barral, Progressive Neutralism: A Philosophical Aspect of American Education [PQS 6].

"Preface," W. Smith, Giovanni Gentile on the Existence of God [PQS 7].

1971

R. Jense, "God after God -- evaluation," Worldmission (NY).

Research and Composition in Philosophy, 2nd ed. [PQS, No. 2].

1972

H.J. Wojtsyska, "Hosius Legate to the Council of Trent, evaluation," PR XVII (Fall 72).

1973

"Preface," J.F. Mitros, Religions: A Select, Classified Bibliography [PQS 8].

1974

Philosophy: A Select, Classified Bibliography..., 2nd ed [PQS, No. 3].

"Preface," G.J. Van Treese, D'Alembert and Frederick the Great: A Study of Their Relationship [PQS, No. 9].

1975

"The Difference in Religions and Philosophy versus Absolute Values," p. 43 in Abstracts of Papers to be Presented at Sectional Meetings of the World Philosophy Conference; Delhi, India.

"Contemporary Religious Crisis and Absolute Value," pp. 537-545 in The Centrality of Science and Absolute Values, Vol. I. Proceedings of the Fourth International Conference on the Unity of the Sciences; NY: International Cultural Foundation.

1976

Philosophy: Its Nature, Methods and Basic Sources [PQS, No. 4].

"The Necessity of Absolute Values," The Way of the World (Feb 76), 42-51.

"Report on the Philosophical Conventions in India," PR XXI.

1977

Editor, God in Contemporary Thought: A Philosophical Perspective [PQS, No. 10].

"Introduction to the Problem of God's Existence and His Nature," [PQS, No. 10].

"David Hume on God," pp. 587-614 in PQS, No. 10.

Comments on E. Agazzi's "Science and Metaphysics Confronting Nature," Dialectics and Humanism 4 (Sum 77), 137-140. (Polish Academy of Sciences, Warsaw)

1978

"Contemporary Ecumenism and Unificationism," Proceedings of the Christian Association for Super-denomination, July 78; Seoul, Korea: AS-D.

"Science and Metaphysics Confronting Nature," Dialectics and Humanism IV:137-140.

"God in the Unification Philosophy and Christian Tradition," pp. 220-257 in A Time for Consideration ed. Darroll Bryant and Herbert W. Richardson; NY: Mellen.

"Nova Filosofia: Unifikacjonism," (A New Philosophy: Unificationism) Kongres Polskich Uczonych Zagranicznych (Meeting of Polish Scholars from Abroad), Aug 78; Cracow, Poland: Polonia at Jagiellonian University.

"Contemporary Ecumenism and Unificationism," Interfaith Journal (Seoul, Korea)

"John Paul II: Seen Bridge Between East and West," The News World (NY) (Oct 78).

1979

"Search for Absolute Value in Religions and Philosophy," Journal of Dharma 4 (Jan-Mar 79), 39-46. (Bangalore, India)

"God in Unification Philosophy and Traditional Christianity," The Family (Tokyo) (Sep 79), 101-113, and (Oct 79), 90-101.

"Bog w pojeciu Unifikacjonizmu," (God in Unificationism) Ku Nowej Teodycei (Toward a New Theodicy); Warsaw: Academy of Catholic Theology.

"Contemporary Ecumenism and Unificationism," pp. 48-67, 199-222 in God Who Unifies All Things; Seoul: Christian Association for Interdenomination.

1981

Unificationism: A New Philosophy and Worldview [PQS,

No. 11].

"Human Nature in the Unification View and in the Christian Tradition," pp. 21-51 in Orthodox-Unification Dialogue ed Constantine N. Tsirpanlis; Barrytown, NY: Rose of Sharon.

"The Role of Jesus in Man's Salvation According to Unification Thought and Christian Tradition," pp. 75-97 ibid.

"Unity in Diversity: The Meaning of History in Unificationism," Dialectics and Humanism 8 (Sum 81), 133-144.

"The Significance of Unificationism," The Unification Thought Quarterly (Tokyo) No. 1 (Nov 81), 23-26.

1983

"Dignity of Man in Unificationism and CAUSA," CAUSA International.

"Significance of Unificationism and CAUSA," ibid.

"Meaning of Truth in Unficationism," ibid.

"CAUSA: Its Meaning, Tenets and Prospectives," ibid., tr. into Spanish.

1986

Unificationism, 2nd ed.

1987

"The Significance of Unificationism," Middle East Report I, No. 1 (Spr 87), 9.

"Significance of Unificationism," Unification Thought Quarterly No. 11 (July 87), 70-77.

This listing of course is but the bare ones of a significant and fruitful scholarly career. One could add dozens of lectures in many parts of the world and all the courses taught and all the students who have "sat at his feet." But this would be to "gild the lily." We salute the teacher and the scholar with contributions in the pages to follow.

Henry O. Thompson

Editor

FOOTNOTES

1. Copyright 1965 by the Rev. Raymond John Boughan. Used by permission.

2. Radhakrishnan, "Reply to Critics," p. 817 in The Philosophy of Sarvepalli Radhakrishnan ed Paul Arthur Schilpp; NY: Tudor, 1952. Quoted by Bina Gupta, p. 31, "Radhakrishnan and his Universal Synthesis: A Critical Analysis," paper presented at ICUS XVI; Atlanta, GA: 26-29 Nov 87, pp. 1-31 + 5pp notes.

3. Some sources say the first Master's was an M.A. from the College of Philosophy. One source reverses the second two Masters' and dates them 1945 and 1946. One source refers to the Lublin School of Theology.

SOURCES

Community Leaders in America; Raleigh, NC: News, 1969, p. 173.

Contemporary Authors; Detroit: Gale Research, 1974, Vol. IX-X:582.

Dictionary of International Biography; London: DIB (6th ed, 1969-1970, p. 628), Melrose (7th ed, 1971, p. 746; vol 9, 1973, p. 846).

Directory of American Scholars, 8th ed; NY: Bowker, 1982, p. 354.

Directory of International Biography; London: Artillery Mansions, 6th ed., 1969-70, p. 628; 1973, p. 840.

Directory of the Catholic Theological Society of America; Yonkers, NY: 1965, p. 80; 1969, p. 64; 1972, p. 53.

International Behavioral Scientist; Sadhna Prakeshan, India: Vol. VI, No. 1, p. 98.

International Scholar's Directory; Strassbourg, France: International Scholarly Publishers, 1973, p. 166.

Who's Who in America; Washington, D.C.: Honorary Society, 1975.

Who's Who in American Education, 23rd ed; Hattiesburg, MI: WWAE, 1968, p. 553.

Who's Who in the East, 18th ed; Chicago: Marquis, 1981, p. 505.

The Writer's Directory, 1971-1973; NY: St. Martin's, 1971, p. 277.

FREEDOM, RELIGION, AND SOCIO-LOGIC

Lars Aagaard-Mogensen

In 1741, a fellow countryman of mine, Ludvig Holberg, ironized social liberation by religious talk as follows:

> When I asked the cause of such a sentence [consignment to an asylum], I was informed that he had argued in public about the qualities and nature of God; this is prohibited in these lands where such curious disputes are thought so rash and so stupid that any creature of sound mind could not possibly fall into them. Therefore it is customary for these subtle debaters to be confined to the public house like the insane until they stop raving.[1]

I have earlier professed great confidence in[2] and even argued the cognitive power of the humorous[3] of which the satirical utopia is a genre, of course. And this one contains a robust insight into the relationship between god and social reality (you hardly know which to capitalize these days), an insight receiving, as it were, its almost bicentennial celebration in the Universal Declaration of Human Rights (1948). The latter is now widely believed to capture the essence of the human position and the theme of "spiritual liberation and the social dimensions of religions." Article 18 reads:

> Everyone has the right to freedom of thought, conscience and religion; this right includes freedom to change his religion or belief, and freedom, either alone or in community with others and in public or private, to manifest his religion or belief in teaching, practice, worship and observance.

I think this outlines a deep discrepancy between spiritual liberation and religion when they are both

1

subjected to the rule of socio-logics (a discrepancy not wholly unlike other distortions the latter produce).[4] A discrepancy, if in fact not a conflict between freedoms and religions, is what I wish to bring out here.

Priority

Conflict quite often is sheerly the symptom of misunderstood, unreflected or unclear conceptual priority. At first many would
think, I think, that a first in spiritual life is (so-called) freedom of opinion and expression (Constitution authors certainly seem to think so). Freedom of religion is then thought to follow as a mere corollary therefrom.[5] I shall argue, however, that not only is there a conceptually prior freedom and that "freedom of religion" in no way follows from it, but moreover that the latter is far from a harmless expansion of freedom of belief (if indeed any such "freedom" is sustainable). On the contrary, examination proves it to be rather an obverse of human freedom, spiritual or otherwise. Let me turn directly to the argument for my first point, i.e., that the freedom of opinion or belief is not the prior norm in spiritual matters such as liberation(s?). It is a simple and straightforward argument.

Setting aside the freedom of belief for reasons that will soon be clear, the Article 18 stipulation regarding belief manifestations, because spelled out into "practice, teaching, worship and observance," is a version of the freedom of action including speech action. The stipulation regarding change of religion and belief, no doubt is a version of the freedom of choice. In other words, the freedoms Article 18 grants, it is fair to say, presuppose whatever the freedoms of choice and action presuppose. And it is demonstrated without difficulty that priority does not belong to these freedoms, but must go to a different sort of freedom. Consider the facts of free choice.

In case someone is to choose, one must have at least, at the very least, two options. Minimally, that is, one must know the alternatives of doing or omitting X (where X may be any mental, physical or combined act). Normally one has more options. Left without alternative, the concept of choice does not, cannot apply. But those options are two bits of information.

2

Information therefore is that without which freedom of choice cannot exist and which transmits onto the informed individual the very options of the choice. Unless there is freedom of information, choice is restricted and, hence, not free. Restriction on information, restricts choice. A restricted choice is not a free choice. Only with free information is free choice possible. Hence this freedom's priority, the freedom of information.[6]

Next, consider the freedom of thought as in Article 18. Freedom of thought is the case if one freely thinks what thoughts one thinks. However, that is possible for a person only in case it makes sense to say that one can think or not think any particular thought and not another thought. One must know one thinks this rather than that or not that. Short of being thus informed, the person thinks freely what one in fact does think whatever one thinks - which is absurd. One cannot meaningfully say that anything one happens to think one thinks freely. So, freedom of thought presupposes unrestricted information, presupposes the freedom of information.

If it is ever true, and it no doubt is - as it should be - that one thinks before one acts, the freedom of action, the opposite of sporadic action, is then encompassed with the freedom of choice and of thought. Knowing that what one chooses, i.e., being informed in what one does, is the outcome of choice, is the resultant of freely thinking it over.

It is then plainly evident that no agent of any sort can have freedom of choice, of thought, of action, of speech, of conscience, or whatever, unless there is freedom of information. Whatever must be said of these other "freedoms," fortunately information, as I shall argue next, is free.

Freedom

It is perhaps true that truths vary in various ways. However, some of the truths we know are <u>tough</u> truths. I think "tough" is strikingly accurate for characterizing the quality of these truths.[7] They are information bits, propositions if you like, which are assentable as such, about which, "assentable as such," it is fully sufficient to say that we have no reason whatever not to assent to them. I do not mean that in

3

the sense that it is merely the case that we have presently no reason at hand, or that there might be reasons but we just haven't found them as yet, or that we cannot imagine a reason not to assent. I mean it in the much more robust sense that there is no way of denying them whatever. For instance:

Such a tough truth is the idea that <u>persons are language using beings</u>. A denial, any denial, even the humblest putative denial, of this statement instantly negates, nay, voids itself. If some person were to deny (were to say it is not true) that persons are language users, he has not merely made a queer claim (the queerness of denying, e.g., that one has an accent, because it's only when he speaks). He has in point of fact given away the truth of what he preposterously meant but blatantly failed to deny. His queerness is way beyond the customary logic's self-contradictions. It is not that it is empirically impossible to deny that one uses language either. It is a matter of saying some - thing altogether (rather than nothing), <u>viz.</u>, he mismanaged to say nothing at all.[8] And only "saying absolutely nothing at all" could have affected the truth of the statement. Nothing else could do. All else could do nothing.

Some will consider this argument incomplete on the ground that it is cast in the first and second person only ("I hear you deny"). So it does not clearly rule out that some speaker might state that some third-silent - person is not a language user. But first, I am not (now) out to vindicate personhood for anything anyone happens to call a person or possessor of personality, such as their dogs and cows. It is up to such speakers to substantiate their claims that this person isn't using language, one way or another. Secondly and decisively, saying so <u>about</u> some other individual, rather than actual deni<u>al</u>, is far from saying nothing at all (and hence is included the argument above). The mismanagement of <u>saying</u>, in saying (something better than "about") <u>nothing</u> on behalf of someone is all that is required for the argument to hold. In short, the second person claim on behalf of a third person does not deny persons are language users. Attributive denial doesn't go through, doesn't even touch the issue.

Barely escaping paradox, it is true that one person cannot use language and that a person cannot not

4

use language. Language use is inter-personal, one user
is as much a user as another user. Or, less
artificially worded, one speaker is as much a speaker
as the next. Language use requires persons, but no
person in particular and no particular person. It is
indiscriminate (hardly a drawback). It tolerates any
person or, we may say, no person is excluded from
information on grounds of being a person. That, of
course, is to say that when and if some person is
excluded (or this is attempted) from information some
other reason(s) are operative, reasons consequently
that are not as such acceptable, but need to be made
out to be so if that is possible.

As little as use excludes any particular person,
as little does its contents exclude any particular
person.[9] It surely makes no sense at all to talk about
a thought no one thought. Similarly, it surely makes no
sense to speak of a knowledge, a bit of information, no
one knows, a statement no one made.[10] Suppose we
suppose someone claims to know something, to have a
bit of information ("Ah yes, I know," she says). So you
ask what she knows. Obviously she cannot possibly reply
to you that she does not know (or the supposition
ends). She may evade your question by saying that she
won't tell you or that she won't do so right now
(suggesting later on). But if she never tells you or
anyone in one way or other, why, then she doesn't
know.

I suggest that such a "speaker" not only doesn't
inform us (or refuses to inform us), she even fails to
raise our curiosity. She "says" she knows nothing. "I
don't know what I know" is nonsense. It is not a bit of
information (except of nothing), consequently, anyone
can (still less) sensibly give or receive. Information
no one received exactly as information no one gave
(nothing can't be given) are empty notions. (As
vacuously empty as expressions such as "infant
knowledge.") Another way of putting this is to say that
knowledge, that which is known or the content of
information, the information, is shareable, indeed
eminently so because in fact if not shared by (at least
two) people, it isn't at all (nothing isn't
anything).[11]

This speaker's putative restriction - that's what
it amounts to - a comprehensive restriction on who is
to know, who is to share the information with him-

5

ridiculously even excludes himself. The force of "if he never never tells you or anyone else in one way or another" is exactly that then he cannot tell whether he can tell that which he says he knows (though psychologically it is perfectly possible he believes that he could say what he contends he knows, but as conceptual fact informs us he can only know that he can say it if he does say it). He can't tell if that has any contents at all. Unless he tells, he ultimately has to admit he possesses some untellable contents. But that is admitting to say, a content no one can know, which is no content at all.[12] So his restriction, in the most telling way, is void.

That is to say that information, use and content, tolerates no restriction. Information is immensely tolerant, tolerant par excellence so to say. It excludes no one in particular and no thing in particular. That total exclusion is void.[13] It converts into the assentable proposition that freedom is conceptually prior to restriction. It follows also, that the decision to restrict what was not unrestricted is utterly void. One cannot restrict what is not free (and in anticipation: similarly, one cannot liberate what is not free). Restriction can only be made where no restriction already is (though, as one stupidity invites another, one can of course further tighten a restriction). So if it is possible to restrict information, and it is, this means that information just is unrestrictedly.

As we know it is true, as tough as it comes, that persons are language users, persons just are the opposite of that void, are by their very nature in the freedom of information. Persons, we might say, are of freedom - in a way oaks are of wood. The concept of freedom is prior to the concept of restriction-reversal of which, in understanding or practice, is at the cost of mismanaging personhood altogether, managing only to be not a person. The free person is prior to, is the concept of which is made restricted persons. Freedom of information is, wherefore restrictions possibly exist - but they should not unless we admit to failing to say anything at all. (And there is too much babbling in the world). Frankly, this is an inhuman condition. Freedom of information cannot be hampered without violating what you are, what any and all persons are.[14]

6

Information, then, we may also say, tolerates no one's decision over what anyone can know. Breaches in anyone's freedom, of course, are intolerable. Silencing is the greatest, regimentation a greater, misfortune; lesser ones are too numerous to list. Variously inspired decisions to (gain) control (of) information, whether gentle, firm or deadly, are rightfully suspect and eliminable.

Mind

Appropriately, the above expansion on freedom of information is at the very same time, plainly speaking, much about minds. (By the term "spirit" I think we often mean simply a "mind").[15] So persons are language users. So what? Humans converse, that's what. They talk, discuss, debate, palaver, etc. Conversation is a highly cherished form of intercourse - and whether it be by head or heart, it is an over-all rational activity. It makes sense even from the very beginning when you make conversation.

Conversation serves two mutually enstrengthening human goals: exploration and agreement. Exploration is curiosity in action, climaxing in discovery; agreement is the meeting of minds. Conversation, you may say, is typically responsive (information is typically dispersive, as we saw above). One person talks, the other answers. You are always, by the way you put things, trying to get your companion to see things your way. This is what information and argument are commonly produced to do. In this give-and-take event, I suggest nothing is provided to take (nothing cannot be given) if you are able to deny proffered statements. You may have a ready fashion to go about denying information, rejecting proposals, refusing commands, declining wishes, answering queries, etc. I should grant we need no better indication that some sort of extraneous principle, such as an ideology, a theory, a prejudice, or a tradition,[16] is operative. This governs your participation in this human intercourse (you aren't a freely consenting partner) and prevents you from sharing an insight. But that is only possible as long as there isn't anything to give or take.

Characteristically, you do not deny everything offered to you in information or argument (you may in fact realize your own contribution when your audience

7

fails to dissent, right?). And when people really get at it, that is, when they try real hard to get you to see things their way, what they do is to grasp for a way of putting things so that you cannot deny them. When we converse, we grope for words, often creatively,[17] driving for the others' assent, for a mind meeting - a goal worth much effort.

So what do we do to get there? Well, what do you do? You put your imagination to work, perhaps even over-time, that's it. Your probe gushes ahead of the known. You force yourself way out on a limb, trying to come up with utterances that are assented (i.e., are non-deniable) by your companion. When you succeed (you found you are able to tell), and humans often do, then you two agree, share an insight, something she or maybe you discovered. The situation says it must have been acceptable because "you" kept it. You can then both leap further off from this new vantage point.

Genuine conversation takes place, then, when you have something in mind, something to give or take (and empty minds tend to palaver uninformatively). What takes place, all the same, to discover or get to see things her way, is plainly a change of mind, most likely an enrichment of a mind (dull, dumb, or fixed minds seldom change, seldom take or give). But anything in or out of his mind, which makes a person unreceptive to information (reason or argument), makes him unresponsive in conversation, is then a restraint, a restriction on his mind (makes it less of a mind). It is a kind of torture to a mind to keep it in ignorance. Anything whatever making his intelligence unavailable for reasonings, restraining a person's ability to act humanly and freely is a cruel, inhuman, and degrading treatment. Certainly many traditional beliefs can fairly be said to hamper an opening of a mind, pre-emptying it for all but the most banal, the range where assention collapses into its vulgar clone assentation.

Liberation

As briefly alluded to above, I'm here rapidly approaching the regions of reality "cultivated" by the psycho- and socio-logics, often of religious kinds. And they are a discouragement. Most regrettably, restrictions on information are not mere possibilities, but as very very few fail to see, painful actualities.

8

Social reality as we know it is very nearly tantamount to comprehensive restraint. All kinds of barriers are set up between most of us and various informations. That is why the concept of liberation becomes pressing. If there were no restrictions, the idea of liberation would be absurd. One cannot liberate the free, just as it is conceptually absurd to kill the dead and conceptually outrageous to wetten water or ban "fun" for being a three letter word.

Liberation, as its grammar informs us, is a process which for its start presupposes a condition of unfreedom or restriction. Liberation by whatever suitable means, progresses toward less unfreedom or fewer restrictions, ideally toward total liberty or unrestriction. (And our ethics are concerned with defending, enlarging, and enhancing freedom in the world, and in morals with their implementations). Liberation is removal of one restraint after another (once identified and individuated) such that the end result is no contentual restriction on any mind.[18] In other words, liberations always move toward freedom. Still differently said and truly perhaps even truistically said, toughly enough, they move toward total information until freedom is the case. This is the sense in which minds are liberated, can be the subjects of a state proceeding from a process of liberation. And the sense too in which we may say that humanity enterprises to liberate itself - unless its efforts are diverted knowingly or unknowingly into repetitions, reiterations, or replications of past error,[19] making a masquerade of its humanity. Before turning directly to such distortions, let me brush, against the grain I'm afraid, in the most economical fashion, the alleged freedom of belief and of its attendant manifestation(s). This is by no means a sidestep in this context. It alerts us to a fatal reversion of rights.

Belief

Clearly and arguably, nothing said so far entails freedom of belief, let alone religious belief. Though freedom of thought is contingent on freedom of information, it certainly does not mean that just because one can freely think, mind unrestricted contents, one is therefore free to believe anything one pleases. For the present, it perhaps suffices to point out that uninformed beliefs rule out that there can be any such freedom. For example, it would be pretty peculiar if I believe I am female when in fact I am male. My thoughts would not be free in case so (mis)informed - from which it is also readily seen that information needs no belief. Belief is superfluous, is uncalled for regarding facts, bits of information proper. Nothing becomes information, albeit information about my more or less curiously un- or mis-informed mind, just by being my beliefs. On the contrary, belief requires a content, some thing which I believe -which no doubt just is information of some sort. To claim a right to freedom of belief is as sillily absurd as to claim a right to be stupid, to be ridiculous, or to be ugly.[20] To take seriously testimonial of believers to the effect that experientially this is just what beliefs are, is as absurd as taking a lesbian's expert advice on sexual health. And that is absurd.

Furthermore, a closer inspection of Article 18 makes it clear that freedom to practice belief is something quite unusual. It is rather unusual, if not entirely rare, that one is free to act out what one thinks. It does not take thorough scanning of human folly to see that this is, as is freedom to believe, pandering for privilege rather than right, quite irrationally so. It is contrary to freedom to commit naively or passionately oneself or others to uninformed action which belief manifestation at best is.

Suppose I believe that deep down inside, Sheila van Zipper, my next door neighbor's wife, wants me to seduce her three times a day. Suppose I believe that idiots ought to be eliminated by hand strangulation after torture for three days, weeks, years. It takes very little common sense, even if one were prepared to disregard the reasonings presented above, to ascertain that however firmly, passionately or stubbornly I believe these things, and however tolerantly everyone else grants freedom of belief, no license to manifestation, in practice, teaching, observance, is admissible.

To put it otherwise, it would be extravagantly unusual if I were permitted to act on something just because I believe it. In between belief and action (even speech action such as "Think before you speak" advices) must come - sound - judgment. There is nothing unusual about that. If it is to be a deliberate and

10

responsible action at all, the human kind of activity transcending sheer impulse, re-action or accident, that much is true.[21] That it takes a suspension of judgment to allow free practice of belief underscores, moreover, that it comes to awardance of privilege if upheld. Privileges require a quite different grade of justification, if they ever are justified, than rights.

Perhaps some will say that these beliefs instance beliefs all right, but they are not religious beliefs. Even if we cannot grant freedom of belief, religious beliefs are such as to merit freedom. To accept this suggestion, however, it is incumbent on its proposer(s) to demonstrate admissible and relevant distinctions of beliefs. It seems likely that religious beliefs fare even worse.[22] How far Article 18 shoots over any reasonable goal is abundantly demonstrated by the Jim Jones horrors. It is not the extremity or horror but the misunderstanding I want to bring out.

But also apart from such extremes - though I know of no sane reason to disregard them here or elsewhere- the right/privilege reversal reflects aptly the factual exercise of "freedom of religion." For example, when some claim exemption from the draft on grounds of various, often religious, convictions, obviously what they do is press for privilege, *viz.*, to not fulfill a general social duty.[23] Or similarly, when students of various denominations excuse themselves from classroom or assignment deadlines by similar references to practice, they demand privilege not to perform according to course requirements. None of these and many similar cases, common as they unfortunately are, are exercises of rights. It would not be wrong to refuse their demands. They would not be treated unequally or unfairly by not being excused. Invocations of "freedom of religion and manifestation" manifested in noncompliance as in these cases, operate the ways privileges do, rather than in any recognizable way, the way rights do.[24]

I suppose these distortions could still count as peculiarly individual or group psycho-logical phenomena though with distinct social dimensions. Matters do not get any brighter when we turn to squarely socio-logical regions of reality,[25] to which the remainder of this essay must belong. We will look at the irrealisms to which social reality is subject to, when ideology, fixed ideas and dogmas, thoughtless principle, or second-hand wisdom, is allowed to decide what people can know. Their penetrations are frightfully deep.

Public Pictures - Religious Reality

It is no secret that Christianity bans depictions of both its god and sex. Many other religions do neither.[26] It is hardly ideological accident that it, as nearly all other religions also, seizes upon sexual action, itself a plain and human enough form of life, as a stress point of regulatory pressures.[27] To bring out how deeply socio-logic administers this ban, allow me once again to fetch a principle clue from the comic (fig. 1).

Nothing is sacred to sane humor - which of course is part of its creative versatility. That sex nevertheless has its daily life almost exclusively in that mode is pretty astonishing. That such refinedly indirective ways are merely open to healthy persons for cognitive appraisal, must make use pause. It is the kind of magic, nay, disenchanting terror, witness, which forms and documents exercise over simple, often illiterate, people.[28] I sense in Day's cartoon, embodiment of an entire cultural syndrome essentially connected with christendom's rote informational taboo. I'm only too well aware that one spoils a punch line by explication, a viciness best left to poor jokers. Forgive me for providing a narration, brief but full enough for pointing up this particular irrealism.

Day takes us to the art museum. This is itself a curious enough phenomenon.[29] It is just before closing time when guards make the rounds to usher out two sorts of visitors: those who worship art, and those who got lost in the galleries. On this ordinary day, the hat-in-hand gentleman is both: lost in a worshipping relationship to a nude. The tone of this guard suggests this is not a first encounter. The customer is a regular die hard or at least has spent a fair amount of time in this preferred gallery. How did the gentleman become "Mac" and deserving of such a disrespectful tone -recognizably for a wide audience as cartoons have? The punch trades on the fact that any custodian knows, that any schoolgirl in fact is supposed to know, that anyone absorbedly interested in nudes, as we are to imagine Mac here is, has failed artistic sincerity. He is more probably a sex maniac, a

"All right, Mac. Break it up."

figure 1

(Drawn by Joyce E. Thompson
from a cartoon by Chon Day)

pervert who managed to pervert his mania into socially
accepted art worship, at least on this occasion. Not
all dirty old men are so lucky. Mac-ania is an outcast
of sorts who, captivated by the syndrome under covert
admission to artism, finds outlet for sexual pleasure
in pictorial stimulation. For this particularly
complicated version of the syndrome, it is understood
that social pressures have deprived our poor Mac of
straight forward eroticism. This in turn is relegated
to a surrogate for manifestation of abnormal sexuality.
That Mac is weak, to get pushed so far, makes him
deplorably ridiculous. The guard adopts, perhaps
unknowingly, this snobbery to give it to him.

It is not only popular lore that endears this
moral nonsense. Scholars presumably in all seriousness,
virtually compete in legitimizing the stigmatization.[30]
They have extensive debates over where to draw proper
borders between nudes, erotic realism, pornography,
erotica, and explicit sexual materials, e.g., for
educational and commercial media. These debates are not
very successful I might add. Debates, irrespective of
outcome or lack of same, wryly evidence and reinforce
the syndrome.[31] We surely cannot praise this crowd of
debaters for its enlightenment.

With the admirably simple means of the line
drawing, this cartoon also shows yet another part of
domination. In the most paradoxical fashion, "Mac," our
fine ordinary citizen, is a victim of uniformed
domination. He has, in a fit of self-sacrifice, no
doubt, conceded restriction on his own access. The
guard can close this public place quite independently
of his decision - he's probably self-employed - much as
the publicly employed police officer can harass,
irritate or fine the citizen. That is how one gets
one's money's worth in the society regulated by the
traditional virtue of self-restraint. Erotic icons are
not the only domain where the single most important
feature is that people feel constrained to object. The
spur of genuine social cohesion is damaged if rules,
laws and their likes are allowed to govern minds-
mistaking discipline for agreement.

Diversification of distorted image reception is
further diverted, in fact entirely dominated, by the
sexless maxim. It cripples proper acknowledgment of
freedoms and rights. As it happens, the art world is
not alone in offering mute victims for this folly. The

14

masquerade includes resultants such as the combination of the queer holes in our movies and the rating system regarding movies. The unrealistic editing codes of motion pictures, and stills too for that matter, fade-outs when lovers unite, cover-ups toward camera enter/exit baths, etc., prohibitions on admissions, etc., show exactly where imagination is presumed to supplant information. These are sheerly so many attempts at exercising control. They decide on behalf of general audiences, supposedly informed citizens. That our closets, media, mail, schoolbooks, libraries, kiosk windows and counters are sorted through with diligence and tightlipped scrutiny, is merely the headless top of the same crazeberg.[32] It generates vigilante prude cohorts complete with centurions, foot-sloggers, landlubbers and the rest,[33] terrorizing the countryside of human minds.

I cannot omit a focus on, speaking societally, the worst of them. Some call it accommodation of parents' rights, some call it protection, some call it censorship, etc. But it is downright wrong. That it is furthermore deliberate and wilfully executed, makes it plain evil. Our image repertory come in two sorts (of course an oversimplification typical of tributes serving subversive causes). One is for adults and one for children. The prudes do not mean it for they think some adult stuff is not for adults either. They would much rather we all become children (again?). Parents think they are entitled to cripple their children's future. This is the most cruel misunderstanding of the concept of minds (cf. above). Minds do not come straight, bent, or even curly, while they may be absorbing, curious, and explosive. The inclination - on whatever justificatory speculations - "to straighten them out," aligning them with one's own, is the most peculiar way of passing on one's own inadequacies or as religious lingo has it, "imperfections." It is a gutless reaction, the most inhuman way to treat a human mind. Nonetheless, whole schools of educators have messed up our children's lives. Gearing learning processes to preferred goals, they have used curricula whose mean virtue was the celebration of these educators' own convictions and ambitions for reforming future minds and societies of minds.[34]

The distance between control and reality, the precision this sort of discrimination endears, is beautifully exemplified in holding words accountable by the number of letters. Word images fare no better, even with a less lively group of great American and other seductive nudes, genders and varieties. The fact is the arbitrarily very very limited selection of 4-letter words (which include after all: live, love, play, etc.) singled out for banning. Moral education as it has generally been practiced is a mock designator for deprivation of information.

The hypocrisy of this can only add to human misery. You have to put up with hours of landscapes and crucifixions to get to your preferred gallery. You have to sit through dozens of sad, silly or sentimental movies to get to the few scenes of amputated interest. You must go (you can to go for many reasons) to the burlesque or live show. Something is lacking if you cannot even go there (not a few communities repress those options). You're lost or deprived.

The syndrome ranges dangerously from garments (dress codes and so-called body language) to the dirty joke and much much further. The pertinent insight is of course that jokes are just jokes, attire just attire. If they are deemed by some audiences as dirty or indecent, those predicates are mere appendages from minds who have turned misinformation into restriction on their own capacities. The sporadic conversion of such deprivations into social pressures, resulting in reality distortions is short sighted, stupid and conducive to human misery, if anything is.

The flaw, the mistake meanwhile must be said to be fairly elementary. Insistence is not at all misplaced on a sharp distinction between judgment and acceptance of information on other grounds. There are several such receptions of information. The most crucial in this connection is neither (dis)pleasing, (dis)approving, nor (dis)liking but arousal, a kind of affective embracement of information. It contains a fair portion of the peculiar sort of sensitivity for sensational gratification which one is deprived of by prohibitive maxims (or at least one thinks so).[35] Prohibitions breed inhibitions. No doubt sexual gratification, thus gutlessly hostiled, is partly visual and visual imagery henceforth triggers inhibitive measures.

The sex act(s), and what goes with it, to many people requires lights down or out. The movies' queer holes transfigure societal reality. Fantasy takes over.

Facts are dislocated by disciplinary whim. I fail to see psychological generalizations, such as that the forbidden attracts interest, do much to explain facts beyond clouding them in comforting slogans. The core, hard or soft, of the matter remains much likelier that disrespect for yourself (mindless mind as it were) is culturally installed. Disrespect of your body or your sensations because they contain the imagery of forbidden kinds, reverts fullness of experience into a kind of shameful reaction - whose essence cannot be disengaged societal dimensions. Whole generations of millions of children, have grown up blocked from such facts as that their parents have a sex life. Many homes have routinized their daily lives, conversations and image worlds to maintain this hypocrisy to mask those facts. Once you can add two and two, it takes nothing short of a distorted, indeed crippled mind to figure out that your own presence is incontrovertible proof that sexual passion is very much a part of their lives and storks are not. Only information can liberate such minds. The plain understanding is truly a distortion of information, a restriction that is too gross.[36] Tolerance is once more short changed. Freedom is denied, violated, curbed or downright damaged. Humanity is threatened.

Final Remarks

I've concentrated on what we may loosely call the entertainment - or the delightful - oppressions of the sexless maxims. What takes the joy out of life, what impoverishes rather than enriches, is wrong and therefore intuitively most suspect. I haven't the slightest doubt that many other areas of image reception exhibit exactly the same dominations. But they would be unbearably tedious to sort out, if not downright depressing, which is no way at all to offer bits for your assent.

I imagine some will take lightly the mixture of argument and suggestion I've given. They may think to themselves one can make too much of the powers of images - the social dimensions of which should never be underestimated. And I agree. Sometimes image makers and brokers have got it all wrong. One word can say much more than a thousand pictures. Picture receptivity no less than of words, can be mislead and distorted in many many ways, certainly more than I have managed to

17

include here. It should not be forgotten that it is pretty much agreed among communication experts that tomorrow is the day of the electronic and other images. But I will not be lightly brushed off. I find it inordinately hard to believe that the image world (also beyond the castrated parts dealt with here) does not mesh effectively with the rest of religious communications.[37] What I've said is a fairly adequate picture of the spoken parts of religious beliefs as well. In a word or three, religious social reality is permeated by hypocrisy, censorship and privilege. It undoubtedly would be to its advantage to cleanse itself if it wishes to take its chances with tomorrow's whiz kids instead of putting its premium on oppressive cleansing of them - or to put it differently, condoning its own stampede of human rights. Such an appalling state of affairs requires that something be done about it. Bad things do not all come to an end unless we put it to them.

FOOTNOTES

1. From Nicolai Klimii Iter subterraneum. I borrowed the translation from J.F. Jones, "Adventures in a Strange Paradise," Orbis Litterarum 35 (1980), 196f. For an introduction to Holberg, see Gerald S. Artgetsinger, Ludvig Holberg's Comedies; Carbondale: University of Southern Illinois, 1983. For his plays, see Argetsinger with Else Mogensen, Holberg's Plays for the Stage; Carbondale, i.p.

2. Among other places, in "Real Art and Constructed Reality," Restant - Review of Semiotic Theories and the Analysis of Texts (Antwerp) 8 (1980), 235-249. Humorous vehicles such as irony, satire and caricature are signs of life. Where they are, there cannot be total identification with a doctrine. In the split between believer and belief, there is room for flashes of understanding, information and discovery.

3. "It's Funny, the Truth is... On Shaftesbury's Common Sense Defense of Humor's Epistemics," The Third International Congress on Humor, Washington, D.C., Aug 82. See The Journal of Comparative Literature and Aesthetics 6 (1983), 13-20.

4. "Innovation on Vanity Fair," pp. 390-392 in Wittgenstein, The Vienna Circle, and Critical Rationalism ed. Hal Berghel, Adolf Hubner & Eckehart Kohler; Vienna: Holder-Pichler-Tempsky, 1979. See pp. 17-33 in Our Art; Gent: Communication & Cognition [C&C],1983.

5. It is extremely unfair to facts, knowledge and information to take for granted that "expression" is always of opinion and furthermore presume that "opinions" are ever religious.

6. This "priority" could be and sometimes is interpreted as conditions of freedom. See, e.g., John Macmurray, Conditions of Freedom; Toronto: University of Toronto, 1972. Obviously, "conditioned freedom" is a contradiction in terms. That sort of interpretation is highly misleading, indeed nonsensical and probably conflates hermeneutics with heuristics. The facts of reasoning and the facts of practiced folly seldom coincide.

7. They are definitely tougher than, though not altogether distant from, "blocking statements," i.e., those statements which are true unless proof to the contrary has been conclusively brought against them. Cf. "The Alleged Ambiguity of 'Work of Art'," The Personalist 56 (1975), 309-315.

8. An accomplishment any old item can perform anytime. If on the other hand, "mismanaging" seems too weak a word, we have to introduce something like a "negative act," which is no mere act of omission, something too artificial to merit inclusion.

9. I disregard the no doubt valid rejection of form/content separations. You will, I trust, recognize the economy thereof in conclusions.

10. Cf. "Has Beardsley Disproved the Identity Thesis?," pp. 138-159 in section 2, Text, Literature and Aesthetics; Amsterdam: Rodopi, 1986.

11. And remember, we trot the rugged grounds where the hoaxy stint of "conversing with oneself" lies far ahead. I don't want to go into the self-deceptions involved in knowing "what god wants you to know" and similar allegorical expressions.

12. It is little to be wondered that the "ineffable" and centuries old debates about it, are inexhaustible. One can say nothing about it (Wittgenstein). Or one can say anything and everything (like the mystics) as one pleases. Babble is just that, unending.

13. "Total exclusion" seems to allow for "selective exclusion" or some such bounded restriction. Due to space and diversionary considerations, I shall not enter that side issue here. Extension of the present argumentation covers it completely.

14. For a supplementary account, see Om tolerance; Grenaa: Humanities, 1978. "Freedom of Information," in Human Rights ed David Gruender, et al.; Tallahassee, i.p. Restant 10 (1982), 241.

15. And here's another reason, in fact the main reason, why I-You considerations appropriately override third person considerations.

16. "About Traditionalist Culturism," Art in Culture

II:131-141; Gent: C&C, 1985.

17. "To Fit Terms to Qualities," together with replies to my critics, <u>Restant</u> 16 (1988).

18. No doubt any new convert will feel his spirit liberated. To throw off old prejudice is gratifying. However, it is a fairly well-known insight that one doctrine replaces another. It is entirely likely that as long as one neeeds doctrine (which takes conversion) only another doctrine can replace a doctrine.

19. "Quotation and Common Sense," pp. 49-61 in <u>Worldmakings' Ways</u>; Gent: ICIWO Press, 1986.

20. Cf. No. 3 above.

21. Cf. "Freedom of Information," No. 14 above.

22. Of course some will object that the word "teach" in Article 18 is not the right word. I agree. We have much more accurate terms for the activities involved, e.g, mission, preach, and the like, usurping manners of speaking on behalf of third parties. This guidance, this teaching, is the muddy ground stifling generations of live, curious children's minds, installing handicaps they must carry, perhaps for the rest of their lives. This has been and will be the order of the day so long as education is left to a handful of enthusiasts who are not inspired to boost the immense power of minds but to exploit the niceties of regulation. The appropriate respect human rights command, and informational tolerance, is matched squarely and exclusively by itself, freedom of information.

23. The draft is chosen here merely because its common status illustrates the point being made without much ado. That it is at the same time a dubious "duty" is another matter. Its heuristic value in context must not be confused with justification, let alone endorsement. On the contrary, see "Gifts for Peace," i.p.

24. Accordingly, religious countries are characterized by their more or less generous giving of privilege to religious practices and institutions and very seldom by their concerns for rights, liberties or freedom.
25. The distance is glaringly apparent when you compare the above with, e.g., Dorothy D. Lee's very accurate

21

"What Kind of Freedom?," pp. 53-58 in Freedom and Culture; Englewood Cliffs, NJ: Prentice-Hall, 1959.

26. A (complementary?) thought-provoking iconological observation can be made on the U.S. Postal Service issuing commemoratives. See Fig. 2. One was on love. Commemoration of love, of course, is symptomatic of disgrace, the supreme anachronism. The Postal Service drew on art by Robert Indiana (1967). For "Freedom of Religion," a pen, a book and a hat had to do (1957). A later theme for love was a flower design, suggesting perhaps love's seasonal or organic worldliness.

27. I don't know whether sex-scare is characteristic of religion as such or not. I can't care much either as long as it is plain fact that it is for one religion and its subsects. God uses the good ones. The bad ones use god. And he created man in his image. Would you like to take a guess at why nudism gets practically the secterial treatment? Why are so-called nude beaches as suspect for ordinary folk as the asylum and the underworld? It extends into art as documented by the fate of a Jesus movie I've described in "Arts and Ends," The Journal of Aesthetics and Art Criticism 41 (1982), 470-471.

28. Apparently it is capable of carrying whole sects. Cf. Johannes Fabian, "Text as Terror: Second Thoughts about Charisma," Social Research 46 (1979), 166-203. See also "Language Learned - Learned Language. A Comparative Study of Text Terror and Humor in Classical and Modern Language Education" (with Else Mogensen), pp. 138-150 in Language Acquisition & Learning: Essays in Educational Pragmatics 2nd ed. M. Spoelders, Fr. v. Besien, F. Lowenthal & Fernand Vandamme; Acco Leuven/Amersfoort: 1985.

29. "The Museumworld," pp. 201-219 in The Idea of the Museum: Philosophical, Artistic and Political Questions; Lewiston, NY: Mellen, 1987.

30. A point hardly in need of documentation. Some recent examples show it still thrives. John Hospers, Understanding the Arts; Englewood Cliffs, NJ: Prentice-Hall, 1982, pp. 335f. Gloria Steinem, "Erotica and Pornography: A Clear and Present Difference," pp. 21-25 in Take Back the Night ed Laura Lederer; NY: Morrow, 1982. George Steiner, "Night Words," pp. 227-236 in The Case Against Pornography ed David Holbrook;

figure 2

(Drawn by Joyce E. Thompson
from U.S. Stamps)

La Salle, IL: Open Court, 1973.

31. Some chase it into advertising. Cf. "PictSextures: A Foxtrot on Subception Hypocrisies," pp. 56-73 in Semiotics of Advertisements: International Studies in Visual Sociology and Visual Anthropology ed Arthur A. Berger; Aachen: Edition Herodet, Rader Verlag, 1986.

32. It is a testimony to the close alliance with ideology that feminist separatists engage in precisely the same iconoclasm (?) on, they claim, independent grounds. Cf. "Field-to-Field Cognitive Illumination: A Case in Instructional Theory and Aesthetic Theory," Theory of Knowledge and Science Policy I:245-254 ed Werner Callebaut, M. de Mey, et al.; Gent: C&C, 1979.

33. Or, if this is not a conspicuous enough measure of a culture off balance in these matters, compare this with the very same movies' wallowing in violence, brutality and bloody atrocities. No bells of intolerance call upon the vigilante censor cohorts to purify such gratifying drama.

34. Cf. No. 19 above and "Detour: How Philosophy Fares," i.p.

35. Ready availability, as in "adult outlets" or mail order firms, is not to be confused with softened prohibition and slackened inhibition.

36. Cf. "Freedom of Information," No. 14 above, part B.

37. This is a concession short of wholesale semiosis. That may be instructive in the hands of a Nelson Goodman. See his Languages of Art; Indianapolis: Hackett, 1976; Ways of Worldmaking; Indianapolis, Hackett, 1978; Of Mind and Other Matters; Cambridge, MA: Harvard, 1985. But there are severe limitations. See "Design Post-Communication Era Art," Restant: Post-Modernism 15 (1987), 131-148.

SELECTIVE BIBLIOGRAPHY

Lars Aagaard-Mogensen, Hvad er Oplysning?; Nyborg: Humanistica, F. Lokkes Forlag, 1976.

J.L. Austin, "Ifs and Cans," Philosophical Papers; Oxford: Clarendon, 1961.

Monroe C. Beardsley, "Shall We Indoctrinate Our Children?," Forum 108, No. 2 (1947).

___, "The Humanities and Human Understanding," pp. 1-31 in The Humanities and the Understanding of Reality ed T.B. Stroup; Lexington: University of Kentucky, 1966.

F.R. Berger, "Pornography, Sex and Censorship," Social Theory and Practice 4 (1977), 189-209.

Wayne C. Booth, Modern Dogma and the Rhetoric of Assent; Chicago: University of Chicago, 1974.

Johannes Fabian, "The Anthropology of Religious Movements: From Explanation to Interpretation," Social Research 46 (1979), 4-35.

Joel Feinberg, Rights, Justice, and the Bounds of Liberty: Essays in Social Philosophy; Princeton: Princeton University, 1980.

John Fisher, "The Problem of Religious Knowledge," His (1955), 9-15.

___, "Aesthetic Experience and Religious Experience," Lier en Boog 3 (1978), 41-52.

Ernest H. Gombrich, In Search of Cultural History; Oxford: Clarendon, 1978.

T.H. Greene, Moral, Aesthetic, and Religious Insight; New Brunswick: Rutgers University, 1957.

Justus Hartnack, Philosophy and Language; Paris: Mouton, 1972.

___, "Human Rights and Cultural Values," Communication and Cognition 14 (1981).

_____, Menneskerettighederne; Haarby: Forlaget i Haarby, 1980.

L.H.H. Horton, "Everything Improved but the Mind," The Technology Review 38 (1935), 1-8.

Aurel Kolnai, Ethics, Value, and Reality; Indianapolis: Hackett, 1978.

Stephen Lukes, Individualism; Oxford: Basil Blackwell, 1979.

K.E. Logstrup, Kunst og etik; Copenhagen: Gyldendal, 1961.

Joseph Margolis, Negativities, The Limits of Life; Columbus, OH: Charles Merrill, 1975.

G.F. McLean, ed., Freedom, Proceedings of the American Catholic Philosophical Association 50 (1976).

Lorin McMackin, Thoughts on Freedom; Carbondale: Southern Illinois University, 1982.

J. David Newell, Philosophy and Common Sense; Washington, D.C.: University Press of America, 1980.

A. Rapaport, Fights, Games and Debates; Ann Arbor: University of Michigan, 1961.

Heydar Reghaby, Philosophy and Freedom; NY: Philosophical Library, 1970.

William Sacksteder, "The Making of Myths," Pacific Philosophy Forum 4 (1965), 3-59.

_____, "The Religious Functions of Myths," Anglican Theological Review (1966), 3-24.

Earl of Shaftesbury, "A Letter Concerning Enthusiasm," Characteristics ed J.M. Robertson; Indianapolis: Bobbs-Merrill, 1964.

G.L. Simons, Pornography Without Prejudice; London: Abelard-Schuman, 1972.

Johannes Slok, Det religiose sprog; Aarhus: Centrum, 1981.

George J. Stack, <u>On Kierkegaard: Philosophical Fragments</u>; Atlantic Highlands, NJ: Humanities Press, 1976.

Aldo Testa, <u>The Dialogic Structure of Language</u>; Urbino: Cappelli Editore, 1970.

Ludwig Wittgenstein, <u>Lectures and Conversations on Aesthetics, Psychology & Religious Belief</u> ed Cyril Barrett; Oxford: Basil Blackwell, 1966.

Paul Ziff, <u>Understanding Understanding</u>; Ithaca, NY: Cornell University, 1972.

WISDOM, MYSTICISM AND NEAR-DEATH EXPERIENCES

Walter Houston Clark

Mysticism

William James once said "The Mother sea and fountainhead of all religions lie in the mystical experiences of the individual. All theologies and all ecclesiasticians are secondary growths superimposed." I agree with James on the important part that mysticism plays in the lives of those who most properly are living religion. Thus we begin by defining mysticism for it is important that the reader understand what the author means by mysticism both in the theological and the wider feeling areas.

In both the theological and the feeling approach to religion there are differences of opinion. To expect that any large number of people would agree with me or one another is hopeless. But at least for clarity's sake, we can look at one definition or a series of them.

Perhaps the best book on mysticism is Mysticism and Philosophy by the late Professor Walter T. Stace of Princeton University.[1] There have been many states of mind and occasions alleged to have given rise to mystical experiences. The interested reader can find them in Stace. He divides them into two groups of common characteristics.

One he calls extrovertive mystical experience. The other and more important type, he calls introvertive mysticism. This is pure consciousness, the One or the Void.

(1) One way in which they differ is that extrovertive mysticism can be considered an incomplete or more concrete form of the mystical state and so less important.

29

The characteristics shared by both forms of mysticism are (2) the more concrete apprehension of the One as an inner subjectivity or life in all things which is nonspatial and nontemporal and (3) brings with it a sense of objectivity or reality, and (4) a sense of blessedness and peace along with (5) a feeling of the holy, the sacred, or the divine, (6) a sense of paradoxicality, and (7) all of which are alleged by mystics to be (8) ineffable.

However, it is important that we should specifically exclude visions and voices from mystical experience since popular opinion often includes them. The great mystics have often been subject to them but have generally held them not to be mystical experiences as such but at best to have been borderline experiences. Stace quotes from the Svetasvatara Upanishad. "As you practice meditation you may see in vision, forms resembling snow, crystal, wind, smoke, fire, lightning, fireflies, the sun, the moon. These are signs that you are on the way to the revelation of Brahman."[2] On the essential point of distinguishing between visions and mystical experiences the Christian mystics and the Hindu mystics are in complete accord.

Near Death Experiences

Here I shift to another kind of knowledge which bears some similarity to traditional mysticism. Numbers of people have "died," e.g., their heart stopped or they stopped breathing, but they were "brought back from the dead" in what is now called a near death experience or NDE. While not unknown from the past, it has become more common, or at least we have some more common knowledge of it today. In part this may be from modern medical science's increasing ability to maintain life in a body that would otherwise die, or to revive the dying with modern resuscitation attempts, mechanical or electrical stimulation of the heart, etc. It could also, of course, be simply that people have been more willing to talk about their NDE but modern medical "miracles" seem to be creating more NDEs.

Here I turn to another volume, Life at Death, a scientific investigation of the Near-Death Experience by Professor Kenneth Ring.[3] The objectives of this book is more scientific than others surveying this subject. Ring spent over a year listening to 102 seriously ill patients who had an NDE.. There was a feeling of "luminous serenity" and "spiritual awakening" in these patients.

The typical NDE involves a pattern that is repeated in many "core experiences." Ring concludes that it is a consistent and remarkable "experiential pattern" surrounding the physical body. After the pronouncement of death by a doctor the typical patient hears a jarring noise and then watches his resuscitation like a spectator. He hears a loud ringing or buzzing and feels himself moving rapidly through a long tunnel outside his own physical body.

After awhile he becomes accustomed to this strange situation. He still has a body but strange and different from the one left behind. Then other things happen. Others come to meet and help him. He glimpses the spirits of those who have already died and a loving spirit, a "being of light," who helps him by playing back the major events of his life. Then he finds himself approaching some sort of barrier, representing the interface between the earthly and the next life. He resists because he prefers the afterlife. He is overwhelmed by intense feelings of joy, love and peace. Despite his attitude, he somehow reunites with his physical body and lives.

When he tries to tell others, he has problems, for he can find no human words to describe such an experience. Also people scoff and he stops talking about it. But the experience affects his life deeply.

At a certain point of the core experience the patient may be offered the choice of returning or going on with the assistance of a flashback to his life. He can clearly think, though on the brink of death, with the sense of peace. This aspect of dying seemed independent of its means. Core experiencers seemed to have developed constructive effects from their experiences with a heightened sense of the spiritual. Even those attempting suicide had "beautiful experiences."

Usually the near-death patients were described by attending doctors as very seriously ill. But the patients felt relaxed. Many had intense experiences bordering on joy. This would be happening at the same time that attendant doctors, other hospital personnel,

31

friends and family members were deeply concerned and grief-stricken.

Though visions of religious figures were not reported often, quite a few of Ring's respondents felt they had talked directly with God. One particular case was a 70 year old woman who had survived a near-death episode triggered by respiratory failure. Because of a medical implant in her throat she had been told she could not receive Communion. She had the typical experience of a trip through a tunnel with a light at the end. She said:

> "I saw Jesus Christ..... I was crying... All of a sudden, I was crying so, I felt something funny and I looked up and saw this light again and it was almost the same light as it was at the end of the tunnel. It was this vivid gold, yellow. And then I saw a form there. And I can see that form now: It had blond-gold hair and it had a beard, a very light beard and a moustache. It had a white garment on. And from this white garment there was all this gold shining. There was a red spot here (she points to her chest), there was a chalice in his hand and he said to me, "You will receive my body within the week," and he went. And I thought to myself, "Well that's funny, that can't be. Did I see something that I shouldn't see? Am I going crazy?" And I told my husband I saw Jesus. He said "Don't tell anyone; they'll think you're losing your mind." And I never did.[4]

People who have had NDEs have often reported changes in their lives after they "returned from the dead." Some of these were religious. Core experiencers reported increased religious feeling involving a sense of being closer to God. They prayed more but took less interest in formal religious services. A global index of religiousness showed core experiencers to be significantly more religious. There was an especially large increase in their conviction that there is life after death. Ring notes that near-death experiences of hell are extremely rare.[5]

These three are the major changes reported by Ring with NDEs. There is (1) an increase in belief in life after death, (2) loss of fear of death and (3) an increase in religiousness. Other researchers such as Drs. Raymond A. Moody, Karlis Osis and Michael B. Sabom have found phenomena similar to these.[6]

Conclusion

I have pointed broadly to what ancient scholars have told us about the core knowledge of mysticism, the basis of all religion. They then invite us to look farther in our search for the significance of our lives. I think it would be profitable both for ourselves and society if we extend the limits of human wisdom through our knowledge of mysticism. That includes both the traditional mysticism reported throughout the ages and this newer kind of mysticism reported in NDEs.

FOOTNOTES

1. Stace, Mystics and Philosophy; Philadelphia: Lippincott, 1960.

2. Ibid., p. 50.

3. Ring, Life at Death; NY: Quill, 1982.

4. Ibid., pp. 59-60.

5. Ibid., p. 193.

6. Moody, Life After Death: The Investigation of a Phenomenon - Survival of Bodily Death; NY: Bantam, 1975. Osis and Erlendur Haraldsson, At the Hour of Death; NY: Avon, 1977. Sabom, Recollections of Death: A Medical Investigation; NY: Harper & Row, 1982. Cf. Also, Ring, Heading Toward Omega: In Search of the Meaning of the Near-Death Experience; NY: Morrow, 1984. Paul Kurtz, "Scientific Evidence Keeps Us in the Here and Now," Psychology Today 22, No. 9 (Sep 88), 15. Paul Perry, "Brushes with Death," ibid., pp. 14, 17. Arthur S. Berger and Henry O. Thompson, eds., Religion and Parapsychology; NY: Rose of Sharon, 1988.

RENDERING UNTO CAESAR: RELIGION AND NATIONALISM

Walter S. Harris

Introduction

Like Virgil, "I sing of warfare..," but not of Aeneas, Hector, Achilles and other pagan heroes at war but of popes, priests, and pastors. And, unlike Virgil, I sing without enthusiasm for war, and I grieve to know that, whatever salvation it may offer, religion holds little promise of saving us from war, because it cannot save us from a major cause of war - nationalism. Since its emergence in the late 18th century, nationalism has become an irresistible force, which Christ, Buddha, Muhammad, and even Marx have failed to seriously challenge in the sense of offering an alternative identity around which large groups crystallize. Moreover, not only have major religions failed to establish a transcendent unity resistent to nationalism, most have served to legitimize national interests. Every war, no matter how it starts, is quickly labeled a just and holy war by clerics on both sides of the conflict. Again and again, Christian soldiers have marched onward against other Christian soldiers, all of them succored in their assurance of virtue by the same faith.

It is questionable, to put it mildly, whether going to war is always a positive test of patriotism or always a negative test of faith in God. Being neither a philosopher nor a theologian, I'll try to resist spinning my wheels in either of these ruts. I'm a social scientist, at least when seen across a large room in dim light - up close, I'm a social theorist, like almost everyone else. This means that all I have to offer is speculation about the following questions: 1) Compared to nationalism, why is religion such a weak bond between individuals? 2) Why is religion-ostensibly transcendent and concerned with matters universal - such a dependable handmaiden of nationalism?

35

Preliminaries

First some preliminaries. By "nationalism" I do not
mean simply a fond attachment to one's homeland but
rather the more severe definition provided by the
Encyclopedia Britannica: "a state of mind in which the
supreme loyalty of the individual is felt to be due to
the nation-state" (or, in the words of the first
national anthem, according to Mel Brooks: "Let 'em all
go to hell except Cave 76!"). I shall also restrict
the word "religion" to mean Christianity, because I at
least know something of its history and belief system,
and because other major religions seem neither more nor
less immune to the fragmenting influence of
nationalism. Also, while I recognize that nationalism
provokes a wide range of attitudes and behaviors toward
people of other countries, I will look only at an
extreme behavior, warfare, because it calls for action
on the part of ordinary citizens and provokes a stand
on the part of religious leaders. Besides, warfare is
contrary to the letter and spirit of the New Testament,
no matter how cleverly it is rationalized by
interpreters ancient and modern.

Let us first look at the relative strengths of
religion and nationalism in bonding people together.
Neither is totally dependable. Nationalism, I will
argue, is stronger, but consider civil wars (the
American Civil War was the greatest conflict in one
hundred years) and the less dramatic civil seething
that itches the trigger fingers of millions of co-
nationalists. I had a north German, neighbor, who
suffered through both world wars and whose husband was
a charter member of the Nazis, who expressed more
contempt toward Bavarians, among whom she lived as a
refugee, than toward the English, French, or even the
Russians, who took over her homeland.

Nevertheless, from Marathon to Viet Nam, and no
doubt to the end of our species, millions of people
have been willing to risk their lives to defend or
enhance that largely arbitrary territory known as "my
country." Many have died for their religious beliefs
as well - one isn't canonized for being chairman of the
building committee - but while their steadfast devotion
is remarkable their numbers are not, even when measured
against one day's casualties on the Somme in World War
I. Indeed, it is easier to get a young man to die for
his country than to walk down Main Street in his

underwear.

But what of unity within religion? I'm sure that between individuals a shared religion tends to enhance rapport; but, by itself, is it a strong bond? In the face of persecution, perhaps it is, maybe even as strong as nationalism. However, it is fair to ask whether religion provides the bond or is simply the occasion for persecution and the persecution provides the bond. Research on in-group/out-group conflict suggests the latter, indicating that persecution is the best elixir for group cohesion.

In the absence of persecution, the power of religion to bond individuals seems to be too slight to withstand competing allegiances, particularly nationalism. To put this to the test, we needn't go to war - just to Scranton, Pennsylvania. There the Catholic churches, all consecrated to the same God and overseen by the same hierarchy, are spoken of without irony as the Polish church, the Italian Church, and the Irish church. It was not a convenient neighborhood identity nor, in the days of the Latin mass, a linguistic identity, but a belligerent national identity that created three distinct churches as waves of immigrants came to the region. Change the nationalities and this story could be told in almost any "melting-pot' city in America, where old national identities remain so important that they endure after death - departed spirits may all go to the same place, but earthly remains go to the Polish cemetery, the French cemetery, etc. European efforts after World War I to make diocesan boundaries coterminous with national boundaries represent recent inroads by nationalism into a once more universal body of believers, but of course Christians were never one, big, happy, international family. The Great Schism itself, leading to the simultaneous establishment of French and Italian Popes, arose not out of theological but national discord, even before France and Italy were distinct nations.

The Protestant churches, spawned as they were by another schism, have been models of disunity - the formula, "99 Protestants equal 100 churches" being only a slight exaggeration. Division based on national identity are less obvious than among Catholics if only because national boundary lines are lost among the myriad of denominational fractures. Claims for unity within any one sect or denomination often can be

37

dismissed like the false harmony of nature-
unharmonious elements die out, or, in the case of
Protestantism, create a new, congenial group of
communicants.

Before getting into possible reasons for the weak
sense of group identity among Christians, it may be
fair to ask whether this is a legitimate criterion by
which to judge the quality or value of any religion.
Perhaps we could even define religion as a bond between
the mortal and the eternal, distinct from competing
bonds of mortal to mortal or self to self. The
relative importance of community to communion waxes
and wanes from time to time and place to place - the
devout Catholic, for instance, may be fulfilled by
contemplative isolation, or the intense social
commitment of a Central American "people's church," or
something in between. Nationalism, in contrast, is by
definition a communal impulse. Shared symbols and the
communality of public worship may distract us from the
essential privacy and even uniqueness of each
individual's spiritual experience. Even the Biblical
stipulation that believers will be known by their
actions could mean not merely kindness toward others
but actions informed by sublime sensibility or
inspiration, whatever form, public or private, they
might take. Even when Christians care for each other,
it may not be for each other's sake but for God's.

Nevertheless, whether Christians are bonded to one
another directly, or, through devotion to the same
deity and higher laws, are bonded indirectly - as
children of the same Father - group cohesion should be
stronger. Why isn't it?

A Suggestion

I believe that the salient continual for
distinguishing religion and nationalism are 1)
concrete-abstract, and 2) vital-optional. Considering
the first, national unity is definitely more concrete
and therefore more compelling than spiritual unity,
even when the latter is cemented to earth with
cathedrals and robed officials. A shared history,
language, culture, and, most importantly, territory
offer a far more substantial foundation for shared
identity than does a shared belief in intangibles,
where both the intangibles and the form of belief are

38

open to endless debate and revision. The range of nationalistic expression is far more restricted and tidy. We're more sure about what our neighbor means by "God bless America!" than what he means by "God."

Certainly Christians, too, share a history, language, and culture - a fact brought home to me, raised a Baptist, when I visited France and felt surprisingly at home among the structures, symbols, and sculpted worthies of 900-year-old Catholic cathedrals. But it is unlikely that anyone speaking of "our history" or "my people," is referring to co-religionists. Given the ambiguity of religious identity, we shouldn't be surprised to find greater rapport - even on a spiritual plane - between an American Catholic and an American Lutheran than between an American Catholic and a Guatemalan Catholic. And this shimmering identity means that we're not at all confident that there are even abstract connections of great significance between "us Christians" and "them Christians." (In fact, the fundamental precept of Protestantism is the individual's right to private interpretation of the scriptures.) And when we gauge our affiliations by the less abstract manifestations of religion - social action and moral proscriptions - we often feel even less matey toward our international co-religionists.

Considering the vital-optional continuum, it by no means trivializes religion to suggest that national security is more essential to an individual's survival and well-being. "My country" means more than just Thomas Jefferson and "The Star Spangled Banner." It means my community, my job, my home, and the day lilies about to blossom in my front yard. Despite presidential urging, I was not willing to fight for my day lilies in Vietnam. But draw the line a little closer and even a subversive slug like me will grab a gun and man the palisades. Though religion, too, is a thing of bricks, mortar, and lilies, it can be exiled from its familiar vineyard without the wrenching sense of loss and displacement felt by citizens of a conquered nation. Being part of us, religion need not be defended with our lives, so the church has no need to institutionalize or coerce self-sacrifice the way a nation must. We more readily risk our lives for our country because it is a fairer trade, considering what is lost to us personally if our country is lost.

Few wars are fought for ideas or ideology, although many are rationalized as such. Even the Crusades were mainly exercises in plunder and dominion. (Distracted by petty nationalism and feudal monkeyshines, the Crusaders only lasting religious accomplishments were the devastation of the Orthodox and Nestorian Christian cultures and the spread of a more rabid and less religiously tolerant Islam.) Northern Ireland presents a more current situation in which religious differences obscure an underlying nationalism. A more profound and subtle form of nationalism striking out from behind a facade of religion is anti-Semitism. As Eugen Rosenstock-Huessy, the late Christian social thinker, wrote in Out of Revolution: Because Jews are transnational and even transepochal, they are "the eternal symbol of life beyond any existing form of government."[1] He quotes a Jewish journalist's reaction to a meeting with Goebbels and Goring:

> They cannot help persecuting us; they are playing Red Indians, and they know that we cannot take their game seriously...They always accuse the Jew of provocation, because although he is quite capable of playing Red Indians out of love for his neighbors, he is incapable of any of their idolatries, and though he can shed his blood for his country, he will always feel that no skyscraper, no man-of-war, no Venus of Cnidos, and no glory of arms is more important than the tears of the widow or the sigh of the orphan. And this is provoking as long as countries must arouse enthusiasm for great patriotic sacrifice.[2]

Bismarck railed against the Jesuits for the same reason, condemning their internationalism and "their renunciation and deliberate subversion of all national ties," and, "the patriotic impulses they seek to destroy and set at naught."[3] In signing the so-called Jesuit Laws in 1872, Kaiser Wilhelm I grunted about the corruption of "our German youth with an unpatriotic spirit of internationalism"[4] - cause enough to expel the Jesuits, who, nevertheless, returned by the hundreds to their fatherland to serve in World War I (about 2000 of these most international of Catholics served on all sides in the war, some as frontline troops but most as chaplains, medics, and, like Father Teilhard de Chardin, stretcher bearers).[5]

In spite of the differences in cohesive power between religion and nationalism, I'm not convinced that nationalism is more successful in winning the hearts and minds of even the devout simply because it draws on more concrete and vital emotions. There is just rarely a need for a citizen to chose between the two. Nationalism triumphs in western countries because it is not now and never has been in conflict with Christianity. Indeed, in war after war - from at least the time of Constantine - Christianity has put itself at the service of nationalism.

There has never been a tradition of Christian pacifism, certainly not since the emergence of Christian kings. (Efforts by medieval popes to limit wars between Christian countries were generally motivated by the need to reserve their armies and resources for fighting non-Christians.) The Apostles were hardly cold in their graves before "Love thy neighbor," "Turn the other cheek," and "Thou shalt not kill" had been buried under layers of qualification and rationalization, most notably by Augustine and his defense of "just wars." (Turning the other cheek was sound advice for a handful of Christians in a powerful, despotic, pagan empire; but with the emergence of Christian kings it seemed the time had come to go beyond precept and example in spreading the light to all nations.)

I don't know how it plays in Latin, but "just war" is a dandy pun in English, aptly describing Augustine's time when both war and Christianity had become commonplace. Even among those early Christians, it isn't likely that the words of peace spoken on the Mount of Olives amounted to a hill of beans in actual practice. Augustine wrote his justification for war at a time when he was caught up in the spirit of an age which saw the promise of a worldwide Christendom as a product of the violent subjugation of non-Christian nations. Today, Augustine's original justification for war would translate as "Kill a Commie for Christ!" Throughout his life he continued to support the idea of just wars, but for a very different reason. They were to be used as a last resort to restrain chaos in a hopelessly benighted human world, which is pretty much our loftiest view of war today.[6]

However, this shift in justification- dissociating the concept of "just war" from "holy war"

41

- removes all appeal to righteousness and leaves only rightness. The latter might quicken the pulse of a Socrates, but most of us need a bit more inspiration to face the give and take of battle. For centuries the church has clung to Augustine's more immature rationale for war and supplied that inspiration. Hitler recognized the connection. When the German Catholic hierarchy expressed fears about the future of Catholic schools under National Socialism, Hitler reassured the bishops. Speaking as a Catholic and putative defender of the faith he said, "From our point of view as representatives of the state, we need believing people...We have need of soldiers, believing soldiers. Believing soldiers are the most valuable ones. They give their all."[7] For perhaps similar reasons, Himmler wrote in 1942, "I will not tolerate in the SS a man who does not believe in God."[8]

Western morality and ethics came to be confused with Christianity. It was inevitable that war - no longer comfortably a bashing-for-bashing's-sake exercise in dominion, plunder, and revenge - while changing none of its basic motives or practices, would at least put on the vestments of divine justice. Perhaps the worst thing to happen to Christianity was its adoption by kings, for the result was more a change in Christianity than a change in the nature of government.

In the 9th century, churches were obligated to support, equip, and, if a bishop or abbot were on hand, command a body of troops. This relationship between church and state seems never to have been questioned. In the later Middle Ages, churches' military responsibility became more purely financial; not surprising since they controlled so much of a region's wealth and power. Yet even then, though the Council at Rheims in 1046 forbade the clergy from bearing arms, it was not uncommon for abbots to have military retinues or lead the occasional burn-and-pillage expedition. (The abbey of Monte Casino made a great fortress for Axis troops in World War II because it was built to be an abbot's fortress a thousand years earlier. Some monasteries were built as unadorned memorials to war-Battle Abbey, built by William the Conqueror in 1066, is perhaps the most famous.)[9] Even the gentle Anselm spent part of his day maintaining knights for the king.

Drawing on the 12th century writings of the

42

Benedictine, Anglo-Norman Odreic Vitalis (1075-1140),
Christopher Holdsworth reports no moral misgivings
about warfare among orthodox Christians and little
support of pacifism except among heretics.   Church
services did include prayers for peace, and killing,
even in war, required penance (the same penance as for
masturbation).   But the major church-sponsored peace
movements of the time - the Peace of God (975) and the
Truce of God (1073) - were honored more in the breach
than the observance, even though they were supposed to
be enforced by anathema and excommunication. However,
even as written, these pronouncements only put
restrictions on who could be killed in war (churchmen,
pilgrims, monks, merchants, ploughman, and women were
to be spared) and when wars could be fought (not in the
several days before and after Christmas and Easter, nor
on feast days, nor between sunset on Wednesday and dawn
on Monday). The church also addressed the conduct of
war, but these efforts, too, such as Urban II's
proscription against the crossbow, altered warfare not
a jot or a tittle.[10]

How could the church hope to limit warfare, asks
Holdsworth. It so conspicuously honored warriors-
providing services of blessing for each knight's sword,
armor, helmet, and banner; canonizing military men,
including George and Sebastian; requiring priests to
accompany soldiers into battle; burying warriors in
especially sacred ground; and generally giving no hint
that one could not be both a good Christian and a good
soldier in a partisan, nationalistic cause, in fact
glorifying the two as double edges of the sword of
righteousness.

While in 1074, William the Conqueror's entire army
was required to do penance and give alms to atone for
the Norman Conquest, in 1095, with urban II's call for
a military expedition to Jerusalem, warfare, at least
against infidels, became an unqualified virtue.   That
the call to arms elicited such a quick response from
every nook and cranny of Christendom (the troops
departed for the Holy Land only nine months after
Urban's declaration) and that the contagion of
enthusiasm was spread not by church officials but by
passionate laymen, suggests that "holy" and "war" are
as volatile a combination as "nitro" and "glycerin."[11]

Violence toward Muslims was justified by Aquinas,
and the Fifth Crusade found even St. Francis in the

43

trenches. The quest for the Holy Land, like any territorial quest, was a kind of idolatry. For Christians, said Luther, the Holy Land should be of no more interest "than the cows of Switzerland."[12] It indicates how little difference in fundamental motives or world-view there was between secular and spiritual princes. Cardinal Cisneros wrote that, "the smell of gunpowder was sweeter than all the perfumes of Arabia."[13] Frederick II, after regaining Jerusalem during the Sixth Crusade, was denounced by the papacy for accomplishing this through negotiations rather than by killing Muslims.

Continuing...

The concept of "just war" once loosed upon the land as a vaguely restricted license to kill is hard enough to control. But try to put a notion like "holy war" back into the bottle after nations, encouraged by their churches, have felt the rush of righteousness - when priests have gotten so used to blessing the troops that it becomes a military tradition and not a religious judgment. What prevents my war from being a holy war, because, of course, I am holier than thou? The notion that God is fighting on our side was aptly ridiculed by Mark Twain in his "War Prayer." But even he perhaps was unaware that the warring Italian states invoked the saints and the Virgin Mary before battles against the papacy.[14]

It is no mystery how God came to be identified with the foreign policy of each nation. God is for goodness and justice and against evil and injustice. We are good and just and our enemies evil and unjust. Ergo, God fights for us and against them. Certainly the Bible feeds such simple-minded ideas as "good nations" and "bad nations." That such ideas live on today in phrases like "City on the Hill" and "evil empire" attests to the enduring appeal of the oh-what-a-good-boy-am-I school of theology. In fact the national ego is thoroughly defended by an invincible casuistry. When we win, it is because God supported us in a just cause. When we lose, our divine status as a nation is not diminished. Paradoxically it is confirmed, for since we are a good nation we are obviously being held up to a higher standard of virtue. It is the sinfulness of individuals - not the injustice of the national cause - that has led to

44

defeat. For example, following the precipitous fall of France in 1940, there was little or no condemnation of the French army or the government. What caused the fall? It was secular schools, lack of religion, unpatriotic teachers, and birth control.[15] As in war, so in the theology of war: the individual is sacrificed to the continued integrity of the nation.

It is no surprise that the state claims divine justification for its actions, but why do the churches - even when faced with a Hitler marching into Czechoslovakia - so enthusiastically concur? The main reason, I'm sure, is that just like "just war" clergy are "just human" - as citizens, when they see the flag and hear the national anthem, their backs stiffen and their hormones go gurgle and slurp. And, since religion is not a 9:00-5:00 thing, when a clergyman marches off toward the flag he must convince himself that his holy robes and his flag are cut from the same cloth. For religion to maintain a separate voice, it would be helpful if an international organization-such as the Catholic Church - randomly assigned senior clergy to posts outside their homelands. Although I'm sure there are many good reasons why the church doesn't do this, it would help avoid the spectacle of a Cardinal Spellman rooting for the Christians bombing Vietnam, or the bishop of London during World War I ranting against the Germans in a manner described as "indistinguishable from the language and sentiments of a cannibal chief."[16]

Being just human, clergy share not only the passions of their co-nationalists but also their weaknesses and fears. It is not a comfortable thing to challenge a nation at war even when the war is a slimy, disagreeable thing as in Vietnam or Central America. Such challenges also may be dangerous, and not only to the individual clergyman but to the church itself. This is not the Middle Ages when the church was a law unto itself, or when clergymen, being heavily represented among the educational and cultural elites, held influential positions in every government. For at least the past 200 years, the Christian churches have existed at the sufferance of the state. This is moreso, ironically, where they hold the dubious status of state churches, but also in countries like the U.S. where the boundary between church and state does not wall off the churches from harassment by the IRS or FBI. Besides direct assaults by the state, the churches must fear that swimming against the current of nationalism could lose them widespread support among the people, even when their stand may be in the best interest of the nation.

The role of the church in time of war is not simple. Is the church a champion of truth, or of compassion, or of the individual's inner peace? In denying support for a nation's wars, should the church deny its sacraments to those building armaments or otherwise helping to prosecute those wars; should it deny its blessing and support - in the form of chaplains and prayer services - to soldiers in the field? How is the line to be drawn between spiritually nurturing warriors and spiritually nurturing war? Should the church be expected to have principles that go beyond the immediate spiritual nurturance of its communicants? Or is that the highest principle? Discussing the ideological issues of the Algerian revolt, Albert Camus, himself an Algerian, stood on the side of the revolutionaries but confessed that he would abandon his revolutionary principles if necessary to save his mother. The immediate needs of a people at war - just or unjust - may require a similar abandonment of principles. (You'll recall that Dante reserved the lowest circle of hell for those who had been disloyal to friends or countrymen.) And yet, how far should the church go in nurturing the souls of soldiers - placing copies of Mein Kampf on the alters of German churches in the 1930s; Italian bishops taking an oath of allegiance to Mussolini's government and the Pope blessing his navy?

In a way, the very nature of religion allows it to play into the hands of the state. Committed to order, it serves to legitimize authority; stressing orthodoxy, it encourages obedience. We should expect clergy, inclined as they are toward texts, laws, precedents, and traditions, to support these in secular forms also. Perhaps religious life draws a disproportionate number of conformers and conservatives, and the reactionary demands of parishioners suppress any lingering revolutionary impulses. Asked how one should worship the gods, the Delphic oracle replied, "According to the laws of your country." It is an enduring and enduringly provocative bit of wisdom.

Modern religious fundamentalism seems to be pushing the cause of reactionary politics much more than the cause of apostolic Christianity, as if it recognized that the main source of passion and energy to be tapped into today is nationalism and not the New Testament. What results is a spiritual impulse unnaturally inflated by a merely spirited impulse, artificially solving the spiritual energy crisis but propelling the culture no farther down the road of brotherhood or general ethical enlightenment. As long as fundamentalists insist on feeding at the same trough as nationalists they should at least remember the admonition: "You are what you eat."

It is the abject nationalism of fundamentalist Christian sects - including "new religions" like the Unification Church - that prodded me to do research and speak on this subject. As a grateful U.S. citizen, I am ashamed that I cause my government so little trouble. But I'm appalled that a major and presumably internationalist institution such as the church, which so confidently intrudes on the private lives of citizens, so rarely finds a voice to address the morality of nations.

Along with Augustine, I feel civilization to be a fragile bridge over chaos, held together during some epochs with only spit and baling wire. I had naively counted on religion to help strengthen that bridge with principles that might lift countries out of that fascination with swaggering nationalism which today could end the world. Not only has my research discouraged such confidence, but I'm afraid the evidence shows churches marching conspicuously close to the front of military parades. So, just as Henry Ford didn't fear the workers of the world uniting, saying he could pay half the workers to kill the other half, governments know that the possibility of co-religionists killing one another is no obstacle in infusing their people with national ambitions. I'm left with the vision of a fragile defense against Gog and Magog (Ezekiel 38-39; Rev. 20:8) - the individual conscience and will. Such individuals can be found within the churches, but only coincidently, just as they can be found inside and outside any number of institutions and probably in percentages no different now than in pagan times.

Toward the Future...

The past is very discouraging, but for a change the present looks a little better, mostly because of a raised consciousness within the Catholic Church. Radical Maryknollers and Jesuits - who know more about Central America than George Schultz ever will - are speaking and working against American policy there. Bishops are thinking beyond the next political prayer breakfast and are reacting to nuclear weapons and the destabilizing excesses of capitalism with principled objections. And the Sanctuary movement is defying the government and, in the best Biblical tradition is tending to some lost sheep. Now, if the Pope would only speak as strongly against the clergy's support of established governments as he has against their involvement in revolutionary liberation movements. Until he does, I'll take heart from the following, which comes from "Clergymen and Conflict 1660-1763" by D. Napthine and W.A. Speck.

> In the furor over the Thanksgiving service for the Falklands conflict [a memorial service rather than a victory service], nobody seriously rebuked the clergy for not asserting that God was on our side in it. Yet between 1660 and 1763 clergymen would have had a field day on such as occasion. A Protestant country renowned for its love of liberty was fighting a just war against a popish nation infamous for its tyrannical regime. At the time of the amphibious operation the weather in the South Atlantic was unusually mild. The Argentinian bombs miraculously failed to detonate. The discrepancy in the numbers slain was almost as remarkable as the casualty figures at Culloden [where in 1746 the fate of the house of Stuart was sealed in a battle that cost the lives of 1000 highlanders but only 50 Hanoverians]. Yet only in praying for those slain on the enemy side were a few wartime sermons of the 18th century comparable to that delivered in St. Paul's in July 1982. Otherwise the differences were so marked as to record a major shift in the thinking of clergymen on conflict in the last three hundred years.[17]

FOOTNOTES

1. Eugen Rosenstock-Huessy, _Out of Revolution_; Norwich, VT: Argo Books, 1938, p. 226.

2. _Ibid_.

3. Manfred Barthel, _The Jesuits_; NY: Morrow, 1984, p. 248.

4. _Ibid_., p. 249.

5. _Ibid_., p. 253.

6. Robert A. Markus, "St. Augustine's Views on the Just War," in _Studies in Church History_, vol. 20, _The Church and War_ ed. Stuart Mews; Oxford: Basil Blackwell, 1983.

7. Ernst Christian Helmsreich, _The German Churches Under Hitler_; Detroit: Wayne State University, 1979, p. 241.

8. _Ibid_., p. 219.

9. G.A. Loud, "The Church, Warfare, and Military Obligation in Norman Italy," in Studies, _op. cit_., pp. 31-45.

10. Christopher J. Holdsworth, "Ideas and Reality: Some Attempts to Control and Defuse War in the Twelfth Century," _ibid_., pp. 59-78.

11. Colin Morris, "Propaganda for War: The Dissemination of the Crusading Ideal in the Twelfth Century," _ibid_., pp. 79-101.

12. Cited in Barthel, _op. cit_., p. 29.

13. Cited in Henry Kamen, "Clerical Violence in Catholic Society: The Hispanic World 1450-1720," Studies, _op. cit_., p. 203.

14. Diana M. Webb, "Cities of God: The Italian Communes at War," _ibid_., pp. 111-127.

15. Gavin White, "The Fall of France," _ibid_., pp. 431-441.

16. Cited in Stuart Mews, "The Sword of the Spirit: A Catholic Cultural Crusade of 1940," ibid., p. 412.

17. D. Napthine and William A. Speck, "Clergymen and Conflict, 1660-1763," ibid., p. 251.

CONFUCIANISM AND THEISM

Philip H. Hwang

Chinese Humanism

Theism, monotheistic or polytheistic, has not been a major trend in the long history of China. Instead, Chinese thought can be characterized, in one word, as humanism - "not the humanism that denies or slights a Supreme Power, but one that professes the unity of man and Heaven."[1] This humanistic tone was already set as early as when the Shang dynasty was overthrown by the Chou dynasty in the year of 1111 B.C., in three different areas.

First, there was a strong faith in Lord (ti), a personal God, in the ancient Shang dynasty (1751-1112 B.C.). He was considered "the supreme anthropomorphic deity who sent blessings or calamities, gave protection in battles, sanctioned undertakings, and passed on the appointment or dismissal of officials."[2] Such belief continued in the early periods of the Chou dynasty (1111-249 B.C.), but the concept of Lord was gradually replaced by the concept of Heaven (ti'en). In its early stages Heaven was perhaps still worshipped by the Chou people as a supreme personal God. We can find such a trace even in the Analects, which is generally accepted as the most reliable book on the sayings and doings of Confucius (551-479 B.C.), when he lamented in times of great distress that "Heaven is destroying me!" (11:8). But this personal power of Heaven was soon supplanted by human efforts and human virtues, and people believed that they could control their destiny by their own acts. Why?

In order to justify their overthrowing the previous dynasty, the founders of the Chou dynasty developed the doctrine of the Mandate of Heaven, a self-existent moral law whose constant and reliable factor was depends, not on the existence of a soul before birth or after death, nor on the whim of a

51

spiritual force, but on his own good deeds. In this way the Chou people argued that although the Shang people had received the mandate to rule, they had forfeited it because they had failed in their duties.[3]

Second, this change from Lord to Heaven also marked a radical change of attitude toward other spiritual beings. "The influence of spiritual beings on man had been almost total, for no important thing could be done without first seeking their approval, but in the Chou their dwelling places were regulated by the rulers," for they strongly believed that spiritual beings could help the virtuous only. It is thus said:

> Kung Chih'ch'i replied, "I have heard that spiritual beings are not endeared to man as such but cleave only to virtue. Therefore it is said in the Book of Chou that "August Heaven has no affections; it helps only the virtuous." It further says, "It is not the millet that has the fragrance (which attracts the spiritual beings). Illustrious virtue alone has the fragrance." (Tso Chuan, Tso's Commentary on the "Spring and Autumn Annals, Duke Hsi, 5th year).[4]

Chan concludes that as the Book of Rites says, "The people of Yin (Shang) honor spiritual beings, serve them, and put them ahead of ceremonies....The people of Chou honor ceremonies and highly value the conferring of favors. They serve the spiritual beings and respect them, but keep them at a distance. They remain near man and loyal to him."[5]

Third, there was also a change of attitude toward ancestors. "During the Shang, great ancestors were either identified with the Lord or considered as mediators through whom requests were made to the Lord. In the Chou, they were still influential but, as in the case of Heaven, their influence was exerted not through their power but through their moral example and inspiration. They were to be respected but to be kept from interfering with human activities."[6] Thus the Book of Odes even states, "Don't you mind your ancestors! Cultivate your Virtues!"[7]

Confucius

Confucius inherited all of these humanistic tendencies

52

and further expanded or elaborated more fully to the extent that his teachings could exert a great influence throughout the whole history of China.[8] Confucius' life as a politician was a failure, as clearly shown in Legge's report on his death scene.

"His end was not impressive, but it was melancholy. He sank behind a cloud. Disappointed hopes made his soul bitter. The great ones of the kingdom had not received his teachings. No wife nor child was by to do kindly offices of affection for him. Nor were the expectations of another life present with him as he passed through the dark valley. He uttered no prayer, and he betrayed no apprehensions. Deep-treasured in his own heart may have been the thought that he had endeavored to serve his generation by the will of God, but he gave no sign."[9]

On the other hand, Confucius'career as teacher was brilliant, to say the least. In fact, "he was the first person in Chinese history to devote his whole life, almost exclusively, to teaching. He sought to inaugurate private education, to open the door of education to all, to offer education for training character instead of for vocation, and to gather around him a group of gentlemen-scholars (thus starting the institution of the literati who have dominated Chinese history and society)."[10]   .

What did he as a great teacher say about Heaven, the only concept that could come close to the Western concept of God, then? Surprisingly, he did not say much. But it seems clear that he did not take Heaven as a supernatural power which could intervene in human affairs. "Does Heaven say anything? The four seasons run through their course and all things are produced. Does Heaven say anything?" (17:19) What did he say about the Way (Tao), the only concept that could come close to the Western concept of God's will? He said that "It is man that can make the Way great, and not the Way that can make man great" (15:28). What did he say about spiritual beings? He said, "Devote yourself earnestly to the duties of man, and respect spiritual beings but keep them at a distance. This may be called wisdom" (6:20). On one occasion he even refused to talk about how to serve the spiritual beings of ancestors. "If we are not yet able to serve man, how can we serve spiritual beings?" (11:11) All these amount to saying that Confucius was thoroughly concerned about this world here and now.

Confucius seemed to take Heaven as "the ultimate creative power which works incessantly in the universe without exhibiting any personal characteristics," and believed that "man is to take Heaven as the model to follow." But his main concern was man's moral commitment and his cultural achievement. This idea was followed by Mencius. But he went one step further and argued that "He who exerts his mind to the utmost knows his nature. He who knows his nature knows Heaven. To preserve one's mind and to nourish one's nature is the way to serve Heaven (7A:1)." Mencius' message here is unmistakable. Not only is there no need to depart from the way of man to realize the way of Heaven but to follow the way of man is the only way to realize the way of Heaven. Mencius thus established the basic model for later Confucian scholars to conceive the close relation between the natural and supernatural, the secular and the sacred.[11]

Liu concludes that "the concept of God as developed in great monotheistic religious such as Christianity had never gotten a chance to take off from the ground in Chinese culture. Whether Heaven can be regarded as a supreme Personal God was simply not an issue that bothered the minds of most Confucian scholars. No wonder that during the Rite Controversy the Jesuit interpretation of Heaven as an equivalent of the Western God was called into question and was finally rejected by church authorities."[12]

A Religion: Yes or No?

What can we make of the fact that Confucians always emphasized "the way of man" rather than "the way of Heaven"? Let me quickly point out two Western misunderstandings. First, some, particularly many devout Christians, conclude from this fact that Confucianism is not a religion but a code of ethics or an ethical system. The Encyclopedia of Religion and Ethics thus states that "Confucianism is a universalistic Animism, polytheistic and polydemonistic,"[13] because...

...there is practically nothing of a religious nature in Confucianism pure and simple....It may

54

be that Confucius has but little sympathy with the religious decadence of his own times and the abuses which were then prevalent, but heevidently considered it no part of his mission to attack them in any iconoclastic spirit, and he preferred to adopt an attitude of strict reticence towards the question of religion, recommending the observanceof the accustomed ritual, but deprecating a too close inquiry into the spiritual phenomena. He evidently regarded the offering of sacrifice as of great subjective value, but professed ignorance of the meaning of the great sacrifice to Shang-ti. He certainly added nothing to the contemporary knowledge of God or of spirits; he had nothing to say with regard to death or hereafter; the "present distress" was a sufficient occasion for the exercise of his disciplinary methods; the present life was the only theatre in which he sought to inspire men to act their part.[14]

In addition, some of these Christians even argue that Confucianism is an ethical system based on common-sense and in this sense it cannot be called a "religious" ethic either. For they believe that only those ethical codes dictated by God or gods, of which the Ten Commandments is a classic example, can be properly called a religious ethic. But, as Kupperman points out clearly, "this is both one-sided and superficial. On the one hand, there are important religions in which a theistic element is negligible or entirely missing (e.g., early Buddhism and Taoism, as well as Confucianism). On the other hand, the scriptures of even highly theistic religions, such as Christianity, may have an ethical content more interesting and less codelike than what was learned at one's mother's knee."[15]

Second, Christianity sees the world as the creation of a transcendent God who rules it through laws. This world moves toward a goal, indeed will end at some definite point and contains elements that are "both separate from human beings' highest aspirations and possibly hostile to them. The Chinese, in contrast, see an uncreated world that does not proceed toward some preordained goal and that lack elements separate from human beings' highest aspirations and hostile to them. The Chinese world is, then, both antitheistic and nonteleological, but everything is part of a larger cosmic process, a monistic whole. That process has neither supernatural authorities above it nor ordained goals to which it moves, but it does have patterns in which all parts of the world, including humans, play and integral role."[16] And as we all know, all these ideas were taught by Confucius directly or indirectly.

From this many Western scholars conclude that Confucius was a man of secular, empirical, rationalistic, utilitarian and, most of all, this-worldly teachings. Waley thus says that the turn toward the this-worldly wa characteristic of the tendencies of the age and not peculiar to Confucius.[17] Yu-lan Fung, in his various precommunist works, takes a more ambiguous position on the question but seems to stress the rationalistic and humanistic aspects, seeing this to be Confucius' defect of one-sidedness.[18] Creel, by citing Max Weber, even argues that Confucius was thoroughly utilitarian: "The factor that makes Confucius unusual, if not unique, is the degree to which he divorced ethics from dependence upon anything outside the ordinary understanding of all intelligent men. Max Weber has said, 'In the absence of all metaphysics and almost all residues of religious anchorage, Confucianism is rationalist to such a fargoing extent that it stands at the extreme boundary of what one might possibly call a religious ethics.' At the same time, Confucianism is more rationalist and sober, in the sense of the absence and rejection of all non-utilitarian yardsticks than any other ethical system, with the possible exception of J. Bentham."[19]

But this conclusion is oversimplification. Although Confucius did not care to talk much about spiritual beings or about the status of life after death, this is only one side of a coin. His true teaching is that man is both rational and magical, natural and supernatural, empirical and superempirical, humanistic and divine, secular and sacred, this-worldly and other-worldly, utilitarian and intentional. His repeated insistence on the distinction between an "inferior man" and a "superior man" testifies to this point well. Smith characterizes Confucius' attitude as "a restrained but affirmative theism" (a misnomer I think):

The extent to which Confucius shifted emphasis from Heaven to Earth should not blind us, however, to the balancing point; namely that he did not sunder man from Heaven altogether. He never repudiated the main outlines of the world view of his time - Heaven and Earth, the divine creative pair, half physical and more-than-physical, ruled over by the supreme Shangti. Reticent as he was about the supernatural, he was not without it. Somewhere in the universe there was a power that was on the side of right. The spread of righteousness was, therefore, a cosmic demand, and "the will of Heaven" the first thing a gentleman would fear.[20]

Towards Understanding

At this point, one might wish to argue that Christianity because of its personality of God is superior to Confucianism, or Confucianism because of its nonpersonality of Heaven is superior to Christianity. But this is a moot point. In the following, I will simply point out some contrasting implications which come out of the presence or absence of a personal deity.

First, the fact that a transcendent deity is present in one culture and absent in the other implies that Christian thought represents open religiosity while Chinese thought represents locative thought. In open religiosity, human fulfillment occurs when one goes beyond normal life to reach a higher realm, for example, a mystical contemplation or life after death. In locative religiosity, however, human fulfillment occurs when one locates oneself properly in the world, in a correct religio-cultural system.[21]

Second, the fact that a transcendent deity is present in one culture and absent in the other also implies that Christians pursue one single dominant goal while Chinese usually pursue many multifaceted inclusive goals. A student who sacrifices all else to become a professor exemplifies the former, whereas a student who desires to become a professor, to have many friends, to be politically active exemplifies the latter. Traditional Christianity insists that the contemplation of God is the only goal to be sought. Although this tradition also argues "both that valuable goods exist in the world and that grace presupposes and perfects nature's various goods, it never questions that the goal of a persons's life should be the beatific vision of God. All other activities are to be ordered toward that goal and, if necessary, sacrificed for it." This is why, for example, Aquinas could recommend Christians remain celibate, if possible, "both as a sign to others of the character of the final state they should seek and will enter if they are good, and as an action more in harmony with God's character and plan than is marriage."[22] In a similar way, Mencius and Hsun Tzu could counsel a reduction of desires, but their fundamental teachings make inconceivable the abandonment of desires represented in the counsel to be celibate or to embrace total poverty. Rather, marriage is one of five important human relationships according to Confucianism, and in this sense everyone should marry and produce offspring.

Third, the fact that a transcendent deity is present in one culture and absent in the other implies that Christians view a person's state after death as important while the Chinese view a person's present state in the world important. The traditional Christian question is not whether man will survive after his death but rather in what state he will survive, namely he will end up in heaven, hell, purgatory or limbo, and this question, as we all know, is closely connected with the fear of death. At this point Westerners might say that "so little concern is shown with one's state after death that one even can question the prominent contemporary notion that a defining human characteristic is the fear of death."[23] But this way of putting it is misleading. The more correct way is to say that the Chinese are so busy with life here and now that they, like Buddhists, have no leisure to indulge in such metaphysical problems. Christians try to "transform" death whereas Confucians and Buddhists simply try to "disarm" it.[24]

Fourth, the final implication of the presence or absence of a transcendent deity is that the most puzzling question Christians have to face is how to defend a just and good God in a world where many unjustified sufferings do exist (theism), while the question Confucians have to face is how to defend an originally good nature of human beings in a world where many corrupted people do exist (humanism). The former is "the problem of evil" or theodicy, and the latter is "the problem of good" or, in Mencius' expressions, how to recover our lost minds.

I have so far described two Western misunderstandings and four comparisons between Christianity and Confucianism. In so doing, I have said that it is pointless to argue whether one religion is superior to the other. But I want to say a few words on the humanistic aspects of Confucianism. Naturally, Christians say that Christianity is humanism par excellence. Christians, for example, always start with the problem of how they can do good rather than evil. But all of such existential questions are solved ultimately by the grace of God. In Christianity the final power comes from God. But in Confucianism all human problems are to be solved or resolved solely by human efforts and cultivation. (Let us not ask which prescription is more correct!) Of course, it may be true that there must be "a help from without" if man is to be saved at all, as clearly suggested by Legge:

> However we may strive after a goal, we do not succeed in reaching it. The more we grow in the knowledge of Christ, and see in him the glory of humanity in its true state, the greater do we feel our own distance to be from it, and that of ourselves we cannot attain it. There is something wrong about us; we need help from without in order to become even what our nature, apart from Revelation, tells us we ought to do.[25]

Again and again, this Christian insistence may be true. Then it should be called, particularly according to the Confucian theory of the rectification of names, a divine humanism, which amounts to no less than a contradiction. Confucianism, in contrast, may be properly called human humanism. On this point, Confucius' own statement, the claim that he is not a creator of new truths but a transmitter of old truths 7:1), has a lot to teach us.

Conclusion

In conclusion I would like to say a few words on the inclusivistic and tolerant attitude of Confucianism versus the exclusivistic and intolerant attitude of Christianity. Christians believe that there is only one way to salvation, and thus the most tolerant attitude they can have is, in Karl Rahner's term, to treat the people of other religions as "potential"

Christians. But this is no solution. For how can there be genuine dialogues among the potential Christians, the potential Buddhists, and the potential Confucianists?

Let us remember Karl Jaspers' insistence that the passage in the Bible - "I am the Way, the Truth, and the Life" - could not have been uttered by Jesus himself, since he accepted all people regardless of sex, position and status, but must have been inserted into the Bible by some later fanatic followers. All roads, if genuine, lead to Rome, directly or indirectly. To insist on the one and only way is to miss the very point Jesus and Confucius tried so hard to teach.[26]

FOOTNOTES

1. Wing-tsit Chan, A Sourcebook in Chinese Philosophy; Princeton: University Press, 1963, p. 3.

2. Ibid., p. 4.

3. Ibid., p. 3.

4. Quoted from Ibid., pp. 11-12.

5. Ibid., p. 4.

6. Ibid., p. 4.
7. Ezra Pound, The Confucian Odes; NY: New Directions, 1959, ode No. 235, "King Wen," pp. 147-149.

8. Cf. "If there is one name with which Chinese culture has been associated, it is Confucius....Chinese reverently speak of him as the First Teacher, not that there were no teacher before him but because he stands above them all in rank. No one claims that he molded Chinese culture single-handed; he himself expressly depreciated his innovations, preferring to regard himself as "a lover of the ancient." This characterization gives him less than his due; it stands as an excellent example of the modesty and reticence he advocated. For though Confucius did not author Chinese cultures, he remains its supreme editor. Winnowing the past, underscoring here, playing down or discarding there, rendering and annotating throughout, he brought his culture to a focus which has remained remarkably distinct for twenty-five centuries." Huston Smith, The Religions of Man; NY: Harper & Row, 1958, p. 160.

9. James Legge, Confucian Analects, The Great Learning, and the Doctrine of the Mean; NY: Dover Publications, 1971, p. 87.

10. Chan, op. cit., p. 17.

11. Shu-hsien Liu, "Commentary: Theism from a Chinese Perspective," Philosophy East and West 28, No. 4 (Oct 68), 413.

12. Ibid., p.413.

13. Jan J. M. De Groot, "Confucian Religion,"

Encyclopedia of Religion and Ethics IV:12-15; NY: Scribner's, 1924.

14. W. Gilbert Walshe, "Confucius," ibid., IV:16-19.

15. Joel J. Kupperman, "Confucius and the Nature of Religious Ethics," Philosophy East and West 21 (Ap 71), 189-190.

16. Lee H. Yearley, "A Comparison Between Classical Chinese Thought and Thomistic Christian Thought," Journal of the American Academy of Religion LI, 3 (1983), 428.

17. Arthur Waley, ed., The Analects of Confucius; NY: Random House, 1938, pp. 32-33.

18. Yu-lan Fung, The Spirit of Chinese Philosophy; London: Kegan Paul, Trench, Trubner, 1948, p. 28.

19. Herrlee G. Creel, Confucius and the Chinese Way; NY: Harper & Row, 1949, p. 120.

20. Smith, op. cit., pp. 190-191.

21. Yearley, op. cit., p. 440.

22. Ibid., p. 444.

23. Ibid., p. 450.

24. Carrin Dunn, Buddha & Jesus: Conversations; Springfield, IL: Templegate, 1975, p. 84.

25. James Legge, The Chinese Classics, Vol. II, The Works of Mencius; Hong Kong: University Press, 1960, pp. 68-69.

26. This paper was prepared for and presented in Committee VII, "In Search for Understanding Among the Monotheistic Religions," Sixteenth International Conference on the Unity of the Sciences, Atlanta, GA, 26-29 Nov 87. c 1987, ICUS.

WISDOM, FAITH, AND REASON

Theodore E. James

Etymologically, philosophy was considered by some of the ancient Greeks as the love of wisdom and the emphasis was placed on wisdom (sophia). Others seem to have concentrated on philos and emphasized the love of wisdom as the most basic human reaction to wisdom evaluated as good. As a matter of fact, some stressed an emotional reaction subsequent to that of the prior love and considered that the desire for wisdom was the most important activity of people. They were convinced that only God was wise and that people should desire and search for wisdom which could not be acquired by them.[1]

The present essay will present the viewpoint of Aristotle regarding wisdom, both theoretical and practical, with appropriate commentaries of St. Thomas Aquinas on these aspects of wisdom. In addition it will show how St. Thomas Aquinas integrated them in reference to some analogous convictions about faith. It is hoped that reason will function as a positive force in directing such a plan to a useful conclusion.

An Historical Background

In the Homeric tradition a person was considered to be wise, to be a sophos, if one had a definite expertise, like knowing how to build a ship, or how to deliver an appropriate speech before the ecclesia, the assembly of the people, or how to pontificate at the religious exercises. Epic and lyric poets, as well as artisans, also, acquired the reputation for being wise.[2]

The traditional 6th century B.C. lists of wise persons (sophoi) emphasized, with the exception of Thales, eminent statesmen or rulers.[3] Their wisdom was of the practical rather than the theoretical type and thus, even in the case of Thales, was not the highest kind of wisdom. Though Thales is considered by the vast majority of historians of philosophy as the first philosopher and even referred to as a philosopher in Aristotle's resume of the Pre-Socratics he would be a philosopher only in the broad sense that he attempted to give a scientific or rational explanation of things rather than a mythopoetic one.[4] It is quite clear that Aristotle did not consider that Thales was a philosopher in the strict sense as presented in the Metaphysics.[5]

Plato in his Defense of Socrates has presented an outstanding eulogy of wisdom personified in Socrates.[6] The older charges accuse him of being a wise man (sophos aner). The oracle of Delphi emphasizes that no one is wiser than Socrates. In order to test[7] this encomium Socrates questions the politicians, who were considered as eminently wise in practical matters, then the poets, and, finally, the artisans. The latter were considered to be closer to Socratic wisdom because they did know the basic principles involved in their craft. The result of the inductive procedure conducted by Socrates is the intellectual understanding that Socrates is wise and that no one is wiser than Socrates.

The nature of wisdom in both the theoretical sense of sophia and the practical sense of phronesis is also discussed in many other works of Plato including Theaetetus, Laws, Charmides, and especially Republic.[8] In fact it may not be inaccurate to assert that wisdom in a positive ingredient in all of Plato's philosophical writings.

Aristotle and Theoretical Wisdom

After making a thorough study of the physical objects of our experience and emphasizing the kind of knowledge we can obtain about them from them, Aristotle terminates the Physics (peri phuseos) by claiming that the ultimate explanation of these objects relates to an eternal mover which is not a magnitude, "has no parts, is not a body, and is completely immovable, one, and eternal."[9] A more extensive and intensive examination of this being is found in Book XII (Lambda) of The Metaphysics, where there is a lengthy discussion of the necessity for an eternal unmoved and immutable substance which is pure actuality and is the ultimate, and most fundamental final cause. In itself it is the pure activity of self-thinking thought or, more precisely "thinking of thinking" (<u>noesis noeseos</u>).[10]

The Study of physical objects in nature is followed by the <u>meta ta phusika</u>, an enquiry into the highest science available to man, one which will fulfill his natural curiosity to its utmost and satisfy his deepest wonder. Beginning with the obvious fact of human experience that all men desire naturally to know, he explains the procedure involved in the acquisition of wisdom. From sense awareness, which delights us in itself, memories are formed and from memory a single experience is produced. Experience is like science and art but differs from them in the fact that it is confined to the individual instances whereas they involve universal judgment. When the judgment is in view of things to be made, or of production, art is involved. When it is a question of contemplative understanding in a special field, the universal judgment pertains to science. When the judgment relates to the first causes and principles of all science there is wisdom. The later stage of human development is the fulfillment of wonder and it requires a great amount of leisure.[11]

Before he goes into a precise analysis of what wisdom is, Aristotle in the <u>Metaphysics</u> calls our attention the fact that a necessary background for the distinction of art and science has been presented in the <u>Ethics</u>.[12] There he tells us that there are five kinds of activities of the soul concerning truth by affirmation or denial: art (<u>techne</u>), scientific knowledge (<u>episteme</u>), prudence (<u>phronesis</u>), wisdom (<u>sophia</u>) and understanding (<u>nous</u>). In contrast with the moral virtues or excellences (<u>aretai</u>) these are intellectual virtues.

Scientific knowledge (<u>episteme</u>) is a quality acquired by repeated activities of the theoretical reason whereby we demonstrate that we know a conclusion based on and derived from previously understood principles. The principles are known by induction and the object of scientific knowledge is necessary and does not admit of variation. In contrast art deals with things that are variable and is essentially a rational quality rightly concerned with making, of bringing into existence a thing which may exist or not, the efficient cause of which is in the artist.

65

Prudence (phronesis) is a rational quality concerned with action in regard to things that are good or bad for human beings and advantageous as means leading to the good life or happiness (eudaimonia). Though both art and prudence are intellectual virtues dealing with variables they are different because art refers to making a product whereas prudence is concerned with rightly orientated action. The terms wisdom and wise are used in regard to the various arts to indicate one who excells in a definite art, such as Pheidias as a sculptor. However, wisdom in the theoretical sense is the most perfect kind of knowledge that includes a true conception of the most basis principles and of the conclusion that necessarily follows from them. Wisdom is the highest knowledge of the most honorable objects, a combination of intelligence (nous) and scientific knowledge (episteme). Intelligence is the intellectual quality by which we apprehend first principles and which makes induction a valid procedure for the acquisition of such knowledge.

In his Commentary on the Metaphysics[3] of Aristotle St. Thomas Aquinas gives a brief summary of the distinction elaborated by Aristotle in his Ethics.[14]

But because the names "wisdom," "science" and "art" have been used indifferently, lest someone should think that these terms are synonymous, he excludes this opinion and refers to his work on morals, i.e., to Book VI of the Ethics, where he has explained the difference between are, wisdom, science, prudence, and understanding. And to give the distinction briefly - wisdom, science and understanding pertain to the speculative part of the soul, which he speaks of in that work as the scientific part of the soul. But they differ in that understanding is the habit of the first principles of demonstration, whereas science has to do with conclusions drawn form subordinate causes, and wisdom with first causes. This is the reason it is spoken of there as the chief science. But prudence and art belong to the practical part of the soul, which reasons about our contingent courses of action. And these also differ; for prudence directs us in actions which do not pass over into some external matter but are perfections of the one acting (which is the reason why

66

prudence is defined in that work as the reasoned plan of things to be done), but art directs us in those productive actions, such as building and cutting, which pass over into external matter (which is the reason why art is defined as the reasoned plan of things to be made).

In the Metaphysics Aristotle also points out that it will be helpful to present the opinions which he holds about the wise person in order to get a precise knowledge about wisdom.[15] First, a person is considered to be wise who has a general knowledge about all things without knowing each individually. Aquinas agrees and adds that it is impossible to have knowledge of every individual thing "since singular things are infinite in number and an infinite number of things cannot be comprehended by the intellect."

Secondly, the wise person is one who can know difficult things which are not easy for the ordinary person to know. Such things are not sensibly perceived by all for sense perception is common to all and easy, and not a matter of wisdom. Aquinas adds that sensory perception is neither a mark nor the office of a wise person. Thirdly, one is considered wise who is more accurately informed about a subject, i.e., more certain than others generally.

Fourthly, one is wise who knows the causes and can teach because of this. For Aquinas these two are crucial for the role of a teacher who is considered to have certitude abut the subject matter he teaches. "Indeed, the certitude of cognition exists when the cognition does not differ in any way form that which is found in the thing but judges about something in the way it is; and because a certain evaluation is had of a thing principally from its cause, so the name of certitude is derived from the relation of the cause to its effect, just as the relation of the cause to the effect is said to be certain when the cause produces the effect infallibly."[16]

Fifthly, as already discussed, that science which is desirable for itself is wisdom for the knowledge itself, is more of the nature of wisdom than that which is desirable for its results, such as regarding the necessities of life or pleasure, adds Aquinas. Sixthly, the superior is more nearly wisdom than the subsidiary; the wise person should give orders, not receive them; nor should he obey others, but the less wise should obey him. Thomas emphasizes that subordinate sciences are directed to superior sciences, "as the art of horsemanship is directed to the military art and the shipbuilder relies on the instructions of the navigator for the kind of form which a ship should have."[17]

Since the knowledge of physical things is the intellectual grasp of their basic principles and causes, it is classified as a wisdom. In fact there are as many individual wisdoms as there are objects or activities known in terms of their basic principles and causes. There are wisdom that are practical and wisdoms that are theoretical, each of which is distinguished from the others by the kind of basic principles and causes involved. In general the practical wisdoms are distinguished from the theoretical because the former are developed in relation to goals to be achieved whereas the latter are concerned with knowledge for its own sake. Practical wisdoms put knowledge to work to reach a definite end or purpose.

Theoretical wisdom is a goal itself. There are three basic kinds of theoretical wisdom: the knowledge of physical things involved in motion and rest; the knowledge of the quantified aspect of physical things; the knowledge of things separable from matter and immutable. These are named by Aristotle as Physics (phusike), mathematics (mathematike), and theology (theologike)."[18] St. Thomas Aquinas not only explains these distinctions in this context but shows how much he evaluates them when he uses them to comment on the De Trinitate of Boethius.

In Question V, article 1 he shows how speculative science is divided into natural, mathematical, and divine. Article 2 explains why natural philosophy is a speculative science. Article 3 does the same for mathematics. Article 4 deals with philosophical theology. Question VI comments on the methods Boethius assigns to the speculative sciences with the emphasis on divine science.[19] Thomas states that theology, or the divine science is so named because God is the principal thing known in it, whereas it is also called metaphysics, "because in the order of learning it comes after the physics" ... and it is called "first philosophy insofar as all the other sciences take their principles from it, and so come after it."[20]

Since there are different kinds of theoretical wisdoms, each concerned with basic principles and causes, is it possible to single out any one of them as the theoretical wisdom par excellence? Is physics or natural philosophy a more perfect kind of knowledge than the others? To reply to these questions, Aristotle presents a lengthy historical survey of the opinions of his predecessors in these matters. In conclusion he judges that physics is not the most perfect of the speculative/theoretical sciences since it is limited in its subject matter and principles of explanation either to the material cause alone or to it and the physical efficent cause.[21]

The mathematicians do not fare much better, not because of their principles, which are valuable for the understanding of the quantitative aspects of natural objects, but because they seem to equate philosophy with mathematics and make numbers and/or geometrical forms the ultimate reality. "Philosophy has become mathematics for modern thinkers ..."[22] Thus the obvious conclusion is that theology, metaphysics, first philosophy is the most perfect kind of wisdom. Thomas agrees that it is "the science of the most honorable and divine things ... and directs all the other sciences since they take their principles from it."[23]

Practical Wisdom: Prudence

After this extensive treatment of speculative wisdom we turn to a consideration of practical wisdom or prudence (phronesis). In The Posterior Analytics[24] Aristotle states that the nature of prudence will be better considered in Ethics, or Moral Philosophy according to the addition by Aquinas. We, of course, remember that prudence was mentioned in Aquinas' commentary on Aristotle's Metaphysics where he says that "Men are prudent inasmuch as they diliberate rationally about what they ought to do. Hence it is said in Book VI of the Ethics that prudence is a rationally regulated plan of things to be done."[25] In the latter place we have seen how practical wisdom differs form the speculative/theoretical virtues.

In The Topics[26] there are remarks by Aristotle that prudence is generally considered as good, that in the view of some it is both virtue (arete) and knowledge (episteme) but it is not universally agreed that prudence is knowledge (episteme). Since Aristotle classifies prudence as a virtue of the practical reason and scientific knowledge (episteme) as a virtue of the theoretical reason he does not equate scientific knowledge as such with prudence, though Aristotle does say that prudence is a knowledge (episteme) of evils, but the word is used in the Sophistical Refutations[27] in a context that would indicate that it is not what Aristotle thinks. In The Ethics we find a categorical statement that prudence is not the same as scientific knowledge (episteme)[28], is opposite to intelligence (nous), and deals with the ultimate particular things which cannot be apprehended by scientific knowledge. Prudence is a precise kind of intellectual excellence that is not the same as intelligence/understanding (nous), or scientific knowledge (episteme), or art (techne), or theoretical wisdom (sophia).

In his approach to the acquisition of a knowledge of what prudence is Aristotle follows his usual method of going to the facts of experience and, as in The Metaphysics, he points out the characteristics which influence our conclusion that someone is wise, either with theoretical wisdom or practical wisdom.[29] It is held to be a sign of a prudent person that one is able to deliberate well about what is good and of advantage to oneself, not just in part, for instance as to what is good for health, but what is advantageous as a means to the good life itself. In the translation used by Aquinas the emphasis is put on the ability to counsel others about the means to the good of the total life of human persons because one who is prudent has the appropriate habit to give good advice in this area. People are considered prudent in a particular area who can reason correctly about what are useful goods for a determined good end because to reason about what is conducive to a bad end is opposed to prudence. So one is totally and absolutely prudent who is well able to advise about what relates to the whole of life. Thus prudence would be a virtue, a good habit, regarding the proper means to be used for the attainment of a good end. It is a habit of action with correct reason regarding the good of man.[30] The prudent person's special function is to counsel well and prudence necessarily has the moral virtues united with it as conserving its principles, because there is required a rightness of appetite to the ends in order that its principles be preserved by it. Prudence is not forgotten by a lack of use but is destroyed by the ceasing of a right desire though as long as such remains prudence is operating.

Prudence is a qualitative perfection of the practical intellect and hence involves a knowledge of general principles but even more so, its primary function is related to particular facts, since it is concerned with action and action deals with particulars. So prudence has a regulative role in reference to the appetite.[31]

A good deliberator deliberates correctly but deliberative excellence is not correctness of scientific knowledge nor of opinion. It is correctness of deliberation as regards what is advantageous arriving at the right conclusion on the right grounds at the right time[32] in reference to good things only. Thus the prudent person when acting with prudence will do what is good and suitable for human happiness, and is the one who is the model for the determination of what constitutes the mean to be observed as regards virtuous activity. From this point of view one can understand the veracity of the statement that one who knows what is good will do good. Such a statement, obviously does not refer to theoretical/speculative knowledge. It does make sense when applied to that practical knowledge, knowledge in action, which is called prudence for prudence is the active quality resulting in a good action, of the individual as individual, as a member of a family, and as a member of the society designated as a state (polis).

Faith

Having presented some of the convictions of Aristotle and St. Thomas Aquinas about the nature and function of wisdom (sophia), a quality of the theoretical intellect, and of prudence (phronesis), a quality of the practical intellect, it remains that something be added about faith.

The word "faith" has been used in various ways in secular and religious literature as well as in general everyday conversations. By many people the words "faith" and "belief" are used as synonyms; by others "belief" is used to indicate a mental acceptance of

71

something as true even though absolute certainty may be absent and "faith" would signify complete, unquestioned acceptance of something as true. In both cases there is a mental acceptance as true of a proposition or statement or declarative sentence based on authority, whether of a person or book, rather than intrinsic objective evidence. It is evident that faith/belief is an intellectual quality different from the intellectual qualities of art, prudence, scientific knowledge, understanding, and theoretical wisdom previously discussed. "Faith" and "belief" are also used to indicate confidence, fidelity, with certainty, trust, reliance, credence, etc. etc. In this essay the emphasis will be placed on religious faith/belief which St. Thomas Aquinas considers as one of the theological virtues.[33]

A survey of the writings of some people classified as "scared or holy writers" indicates that the word fides was used by Matthew and Paul for fidelity which is a virtue of the will indicating constancy in keeping promises and agreements. They use it, also, for veracity (truthfulness), for trust, for a practical judgment for what is to be done, and for the object of faith, as in the Athanasian Creed: "this is the Catholic Faith."[34]

St. Thomas Aquinas begins his examination of faith by pointing out that the object of every cognitive habit includes the material object considered and the formal aspect in which the material is considered. Applying this to faith he concludes that the formal aspect is the First Truth because faith does not assent to anything except because it is revealed by God. Hence faith includes in its subject not only God Himself as revealed but also other things inasmuch as they help people towards the enjoyment of God. Furthermore, since things known are in the knower according to the manner of the knower and the proper manner of the human intellect regards knowing is the judgment or proposition that asserts the truth, the object of faith is expressed not by an idea, which is simple, but by the proposition which is a complex of subject and predicate. Thus faith which is based on the First Truth, God, cannot be expressed in a false statement. Also, since by faith the intellect assents to something not because the intellect is moved thereto by the presence of the object but through an act of choice, the intellect voluntarily turns to the assent without any doubt about its truth.

In answer to the question about the relationship of science and faith, Thomas Aquinas points out that all science is derived from self-evident principles which are directly known whereas faith involves a free assent to what is not so known. So it is impossible for the same thing to be known and believed by the same person at the same time. It can be known and believed by different people at the same time and one person at one time can believe something and later know it by demonstration, as for example the existence of God. Too, one can know that there is a God and believe, at the same time, that that God is a Trinity of Persons.

As is well known, there have been many debates about the contents of the Catholic faith and how precisely those contents should be expressed and what is the ultimate basis for the authority upon which faith is determined. Aquinas points out that the contents of the faith have been expressed in various creeds which have been formulated to make explicit the truth present in the Church from the beginning to set aside certain errors that arose at different times. So a new edition to a creed can be published by the authority empowered to decide matters of faith and that authority is the authority of the Sovereign Pontiff in accord with the statement of Our Lord to Peter (Luke 22:32) and the assertion by Paul "That you all speak the same thing, and that there be no schisms among you" (1 Cor 1:10). This could not be secured unless any question of faith that may arise be decided by him who presides over the whole Church.[35]

After presenting the material and formal objects of faith, since the acts of the intellect are distinguished by their formal objects, Aquinas considers the interior act of faith. It is not the same as intelligence or understanding because what is believed is not understood in itself. It is not theoretical wisdom because not a conclusion from most basic principles naturally known but it is similar to reasoning in that it involves an intellectual enquiry but different because it depends upon an act of the will. Faith is a free act that is formally intellectual and efficiently voluntary involving the cooperative activity of the grace of God: "The act of believing is an act of the intellect assenting to divine truth at the command of the will moved by the grace of God."[36]   Thus " ... two things are required that the act of faith may be perfect: that the intellect should infallibly tend to its object, which is the true, and that the other is that the act should be infallibly directed to its last end, because of which the will assents to the true, ... since nothing false can be the object of faith."[37]

Faith is also more certain than the intellectual virtues of prudence and art since it concerns necessary matters, whereas prudence and art are about the contingent.   It is more certain than wisdom, science, and understanding because it rests upon the divine truth whereas the others rest upon human reason.[38] There are two things essential for faith: it must come form God as regards what is believed and form God as an internal cause moving a person to assent to what belongs to faith.   Faith is the cause in people of filial fear, whereby one dreads to be separated form God, and reverential fear, whereby one submits his intellect to God so as to believe in all the divine promises.

It may be appropriate to terminate this essay by a consideration of some of the gifts of the Holy Spirit which accompany faith.   The gift of understanding is a gift by which the Holy Spirit illumines the human mind so that it know a definite supernatural truth toward which a right will should tend.   The gift of science is a gift of the Holy Spirit aiding in the ordering of the human intellect in the use of human reasons whereas the gift of wisdom refers to divine reasons and is a perfection of the human mind according to which it is disposed to follow the inspiration of the Holy Spirit in the knowledge of either the divine or the human. The gift of counsel aids in the application of knowledge to individual activities regarding the prudential choice of the appropriate means to secure their due end.[39]

1. Diogenes Laertius, Lives of Eminent Philosophers tr Robert D. Hicks; NY: Putnam, 1925, vol. I.12. Diogenes Laertius asserts that the first one to call himself a philosopher or lover of wisdom was Pythagoras "for he said no man is wise but God alone." This seems to be echoed by Plato in his Defense of Socrates, (Apol. 23a5) "... but the truth is, o Men of Athens, that God only is wise;" Jowett translation. Diogenes also states that "Sophists was another name for the wise men, and not only for philosophers but for the poets, also, and so Cratinus when praising Homer and Hesiod in his Archilochi gives them the title of sophist." Ibid., Diogenes states in IX, 69-70 that "Skeptics were called such because they were always looking for truth and never finding it." Something similar is found in "The Outlines of Pyrrhonism," by Sextus Empiricus.

2. Homer, Iliad, Bk. 15, 412. Solon, "The Poet's Soliloquy," line, 52, Greek Lyric Poetry by David A. Campbell; NY: St. Martin's Press, 1967.

3. Diogenes Laertius, ibid., I, 13.

4. Geoffrey S. Kirk and John E. Raven, The Presocratic Philosophers; Cambridge: University Press, 1960, p. 98, "Thales evidently abandoned mythic formulations: this alone justifies the claims that he was the first philosopher, naive though his thought still was." How one can evaluate his formulations, mythic or otherwise, if he "did not write a book," op. cit., p. 86, is difficult to understand. Reginald E. Allen, Greek Philosophy: Thales to Aristotle, 2nd ed; NY: Free Press, 1985, p. 1, "Every history of philosophy begins with Thales..." This is a question-statement if one takes seriously what Diogenes says, "But philosophy, the pursuit of wisdom, has had a twofold origin; it started with Anaximander on the one hand, with Pythagoras on the other," op. cit., p. 13. Herodotus (I.30) calls Solon a lover of knowledge in a general sense seeking a theoretical knowledge of all things.

5. 1026 a 18-20.

6. Is the Apology an attempt to show that Socrates is really a wise man, the model for all philosophers? There are at least 45 places where Plato uses the word

"wisdom" or "wise" or the comparative or superlative degree of the adjective.

7. John Burnet states that Socrates tried to prove that the god was a liar (note to 21b8 in Plato's Euthyphro Apology of Socrates and Crito; Oxford: Clarendon Press, 1924, p. 92). Arthur E. Taylor states that "Socrates says that he was at first staggered by this pronouncement, and set to work to prove Apollo of Delphi - never a persona grata at Athens, for excellent reasons - a liar." Plato: The Man and His Work; NY: Meridian Books, 1958, p. 161. If this were the case, how could Socrates say, "He certainly cannot be lying, for that is impossible for him." "Would it not be an admission of atheism to try to prove that Apollo was a liar? Is it not the case that Socrates is presented by Plato as using the "second best proof" which is here the accumulation of evidence to verify the hypothesis and prove that Socrates is really the wisest of men?

8. Smile of the Line, 509d6-511e5; myth of the Cave, 514a1-518d.

9. Physics Bk. 8; Aristotle Dictionary ed Thomas P. Kiernan, "Introduction to the Aristotelian Writings," Theodore E. James, p. 76.

10. Meta. 1072b 29-30; 2074n 35.

11. James, op. cit., p. 111.

12. Eth. Nich. VI, 1139 b 15 ff.

13. Meta. 981b 26 ff.

14. In Duodecim Libros Metaphysicorum Aristotelis Expositio; Taurini/Romae: Marietti, 1950, L.I. 1. 34, p. 11; English tr John P. Rowan, Library of Living Catholic Thought, vol. I; Chicago: Regnery, 1961, p. 16. Eth. Nich., cf. n. 12.

15. Aristotle, Meta. 982a 6ff. Aquinas, Comm., pp. 18-19.

16. Aristotle, Meta. 981b 8-9. Aquinas, S. Theol. II,II,Q.18, a. 4c; I.Q.22. a.1 ad 1; I. II. Q.40,a.2 ad 3; 3 Sent. 23.2.2.3c and 26.2.4c. De Veritate Q. XI, On The Teacher.

17. Aquinas, Comm. Meta. of Aristotle, I. L.2, Rowan tr, vol. I, p.19.

18. Aristotle, Meta. 1026a 8-21, esp. 18-20. Aquinas, Comm., nos. 1145-1170.

19. Aristotle, Meta. 983b 4ff, 988a 18ff. Aristotle's criticism of his predecessors may have some value today in reference to the positivists, logical or otherwise, and the scientificosecular humanists. St. Thomas Aquinas: The Division and Methods of the Sciences, Questions V and VI of his Commentary on the De Trinitate of Boethius, tr with Introduction and Notes, by Armand Maurer, C.S.B.; Toronto: Pontifical Institute of Medieval Studies, 1953.

20. Maurer, op. cit., p. 8.

21. Note 19.

22. Meta. 985b 25; 992a 31-b 1; 1036b 12.

23. S. Thomae Aquinatis In Dec Libros Ethicorum Aristotelis Ad Nicomachum Expositio, cura et studio P. Fr. Raymundi M. Spiazzi, O.P.; Taurini/Romae: Marietti, 1949, tr C.I. Litzinger, O.P., Library of Living Catholic Thought; Chicago: Regnery, 1964, vol. 1:569.

24. Aristotle, Post. Anal. 89b8.

25. Aristotle, Meta. 980b 22. Aquinas, Comm., op. cit. vol. I:10.

26. Topic 119b 33; 121b 31; 136b 11; 145a 28-32

27. 18a 8.

28. Eth. Nich. 1142a24ff.

29. Ibid., 1140a 24ff.

30. Comm. in Eth. Nich., op. cit. L. VI, Lect. IV, 1171. Aristotle, Eth. Nich. 1140b 20-22

31. Eth. Nich. 1141b 14-21; 1142a 14. Aquinas, Comm. nos 1194/1208.

32. Eth. Nich. 1142b-1143a. Aquinas, Comm, 1217ff.

33. S. Theol. II.II, Q.1.a.1, Introduction to Pecci ed; Paris: 1888.

34. Ibid., Pecci ed. footnote.

35. S. Theol. II.II.Q.1.a.10, Pecci ed, Vol. 3, p. 23. Anton C. Pegis, ed., Basic Writings of St. Thomas Aquinas; NY: Random House, 1945, Vol. 2:1073.

36. Ibid., Q. 2. a. 9c, Pecci ed, p. 33. Pegis, op. cit., pp. 1087-1088.

37. Ibid., Q.4. a 5c, Pecci ed. p. 42. Pegis, op. cit., p. 1102.

38. Ibid., Q. 4, a.8c, Pecci ed. p. 42. Pegis, op. cit., p. 1106.

39. For the locations of additional information about the gifts of the Holy Spirit consult Roy J. Deferrari, Sister M. Inviolata Barry, and Ignatius Mcguiness, A Lexicon of St. Thomas Aquinas; Washington: Catholic University of America, 1949, under heading donum, pp. 342.3.

THE WISDOM OF ISLAM IN SUFISM

Yasar Nuri Ozturk

Islamic mysticism is the interpretation favored by western writers as a translation of the Arabic tasawwuf. There are several translations for this word but mysticism is best when the intent is to share what is in common with other forms of mysticism. Here one includes the question of human origin and destiny coupled with a longing of the soul for immediate contact with the ground of its existence. But in pointing to this common concern, the phrase "Islamic Mysticism" points away from the uniqueness of tasawwuf. It implies a universal question but it also proposes a unique answer to it. To emphasize this uniqueness, I use a word originally coined in Germany in the 19th century. "Sufism" has gained wide currency in English and among Muslims as well.

What is Mysticism?

From time immemorial, the human spirit has had a longing for contact with the essence of existence. People have exerted themselves to the limits of their capacity to achieve this contact. The yearning for such a contact is deep in the human spirit. This is the goal of almost all mystics. Pascal said "L'immensite de ces espaces infinies m'effraie." "The immensity of these infinite spaces frightens me."[1] The main reason for this fright is the deep separation of mankind from the Creator, the source of the human spirit. Some of the great works of the sufis are on this subject. Here are such writings as Mathnawi by the famous Turkish mystic poet, Rumi (d. 1272)), and the Javidnama of the contemporary mystic poet, Muhammed Iqbal (d. 1938). Iqbal has been called the Rumi of today. In the introduction of his monumental Javidnama, he said:

> Man, in this world of seven hues
> Lute-like is ever afire with lamentation

79

Yearning for a kindred spirit burns him
inwardly
Teaching him the remedies to soothe the
heart...[2]

A body of thought has emerged from these efforts.
There is a form and an approach by which contact is
made possible, by which human thirst for divine union
is satisfied. This is mysticism. We can say that
"Mysticism is essentially one and the same, whatever
may be the religion professed by individual mystics. It
is a constant and unvarying phenomenon of the universal
yearning of the human spirit for personal communion
with God."[3] "All mystics feel the same, but they say
different things."[4] "It may be said that all mystical
experience ultimately meets in a single point, but that
point assumes widely different aspects according to the
mystic's religion, race and temperament. . ."[5] In a
word, "mysticism, according to its historical and
psychological definitions, is the direct intuition or
experience of God."[6]

Mystical contemplation and the search for mystical
union reach back to the dawn of time. They will remain
features of human life until the sunset of man's
existence. This search has not always been obvious. It
has manifested itself in a great variety of activities
including art, love, adventure and even rebellion. But
an investigation of all these phenomena reveals that
they spring from a common end, contact with the
creative and sustaining power at the heart of things.
So it is that the motivating force underlying all human
progress, all human institutions including religion, is
discovered to be mystical yearning. If religion is the
wellspring of civilization and this is virtually
indisputable, then clearly this longing and the
reflection it produces must rate foremost among the
creative powers of mankind. They lie at the heart of
religion and those religions which don't possess them
in their hearts possess neither the power to influence
human history nor the capacity to survive for long.

Hence, every religion has or must have two areas
or doctrines, absolute and relative, although the
language of these areas differs from one to another.
The absolute one which characterizes esoteric doctrine
of the religion is called, generally, mysticism. The
other which characterizes exoteric doctrine, is called
law or, generally speaking, morality.

The development of mystical sensibilities in man is basic to the history of religions. However, these sensibilities have not always existed to the same degree in all men. Hence, there has arisen in the religious history of man a field of knowledge not accessible to all - a "secret field," a secret wisdom, requiring initiation. It addresses itself to those in whom mystical sensibilities are more highly developed. Mundane religion addresses itself to all in terms understandable to all. Above and beyond the mundane there is an infinite field of spirituality, knowledge and divine wisdom apprehendable by more mature personalities. It is a field which cannot be desultorily opened to all. Its secrets, its principles, and the training necessary to grasp them can be shared only with persons sufficiently developed to be receptive to them. Herein lies the meaning of "mysticism," a word to be derived from the Latin mysterium meaning "to close the eyes and lips, to be secret." The name mysticism, as Margaret Smith pointed out, "is historically connected with the mystery-cults of the Greeks. The mystic was one who had been initiated into the secret knowledge of divine things, and was under the obligation to keep silence concerning the knowledge which had been imparted to him. The term mystical could be applied to any esoteric doctrine which was revealed only to the initiated...[7]

A process of initiation has long been a requirement of mystical thought and training. Its importance in Sufism is revealed by history. After an extended period, of about five centuries, the rigorousness of initiation was lightened and the gates to Sufism were opened to the masses. The result was often tragic. Those who entered through these gates were unable to digest what lay beyond. Many lives were lost and there was much criticism and antagonism. It is a fact of life that no matter how far one has gone, there will be those who have gone further, and one person who has gone furthest. The advanced persons will be subject to criticism and enmity. Those who go before see things invisible to those who from behind. Thus they will always be considered strange and evoke jealousy. Under these circumstances, it becomes necessary to reveal some things only with great care and others not at all.

Margaret Smith summed up the postulates of

81

mysticism.[8]

1. A unique mode of perception
2. Having an inward and divine light
3. Purification from self
4. Love
5. Union with God.

What is Sufism?

It is known that one of the most difficult things in human life is to give a clear definition of spiritual experiences, especially for a man who travels in the immense realm of the spirit and receives a direct relation with the essence of the universe. That is why I appreciate the explanation of Nicholson.

> All symbolic descriptions of union with God and theories concerning its nature are little better than leaps in the dark... Whatever terms may be used to describe it, the intuitive state is the culmination of the simplifying process by which the soul is gradually isolated from all that is foreign to itself, from all that is not God.[9]

Hence, it is not easy as it is for the other disciplines to define mysticism in general and sufism in particular. Every mystic can give a definition in accordance with his or her own experience and level. This strict relativity can be seen in sufi literature, in which we meet hundreds of definitions concerning sufism or sufi. We present only some examples.[10] Junayd of Baghdad (298 A.H./910 A.D.) is known as the "master of Sufis."

> Sufism is the purification of the heart from associating with created beings, separation from natural characteristics, suppression of human qualities, avoiding the temptations of the carnal soul, taking up the qualities of the spirit, attachment to the sciences of reality, using what is more proper to the eternal, counselling all the community, being truly faithful to God, and following the Prophet according to the law.

Abu'l-Husayn an Nuri's (295/908) definition is that "Sufism is abandoning all the portion of the carnal soul." Sahl b. Abdullah at-Tustary (208/896), being

82

asked what a sufi is, replied, "One who is clean of impurity, full of meditation; who is cut off from humanity for God's sake, and in whose eyes gold and mud are equal." Sumnun al-Muhasibi said "Sufism is that you possess everything while nothing can possess you." According to Kattani (322/933), "Sufism is nothing but morality." Shibli (334/945) claimed "Sufism is a friendly relationship with God." Ruzbari maintained that "Sufism is striving and zeal." According to the famous Turkish Sufi, Abdulhakim Arvasi (d. 1949), "Sufism is the interior character of the divine law, Sharia."[11]

Many writers, taking as their point of departure one or another of the customary classifications, have found it possible to categorize sufism as this or that type of mysticism. However, such an approach does immediate violence to the integrity of sufism. Sufism must be considered a <u>sui generis</u> (unique) discipline. Indian, Christian and Neoplatonic forms of mysticism, among others, in spite of the issues and concepts they share in common with this discipline, are different systems. In taking the human soul, God, life and religious narratives as fundamental, these systems do, of course, exhibit points of correspondence with sufism. The mystical approach and mystical thought are, after all, part of the common heritage and inclination of mankind. However, it is wrong to assume that points of correspondence between complex and otherwise dissimilar doctrines means these elements have been borrowed. This reductionist assumption and its application contribute little to an understanding of sufism.

Above all, sufism is a religious mysticism. In this respect, it must be distinguished immediately from Neoplatonism which is a philosophic mysticism.

We must ask again, "What is Sufism?" It is an Islamic institution, rooted in revelation, molded in the image of the Prophet, and addressed to the mystical bent and needs of man. So, sufism is neither a philosophy, because it is based on revelation, nor an independent religion, because its sources are the Quran and the Prophet's tradition. It is necessary to understand the definition presented by Nicholson that "Sufism is the religious philosophy of Islam" as a meaning which depends on sufism being Islamic.[12]

Western scholars and authors have been trying to show sufism comes from outside of Islam. They have tried to find some artificial "background." Almost all of them seem to be concentrating on inventing or producing some so-called influences on this Islamic institution.

The religion of sufism is Islam. Sufism is the esoteric interpretation of Islam. A sufi is a disciple of the Quran and Sunna before being a philosopher or poet. It is after this necessary acceptance that we can participate in the great orientalist Arberry's phrase. "Sufism may be defined as the mystical movement of an uncompromising monotheism."[13]

In conclusion, sufism depends on the Quran and the Sunna, the Tradition of the Prophet.

How it Works

The dominant character of sufism is <u>action</u>. It is a mysticism of action, sensitive to the Quran's insistence that man produce works. These are not simply works understood as acts of worship in religion, but works understood broadly as participation in the creative activity of God. In sufism, God is not a being outside of existence who observes, from afar, a work which has been completed. In every moment, existence trembles and is transformed as a manifestation of God Himself. "Every day He exercises universal power" says the Quran.[14] Thus contact with the ground of existence is not to be realized beyond existence, but through an active engagement with it. A sufi is one who has ceased to be a passive observer of existence and has become an active participant in its creation.

Herein lies the fundamental difference between the <u>moksha</u> of Indian mysticism, and Sufism's concept of <u>fana</u> (annihilation, transmutation of self, passing away of individual self in universal being). The <u>moksha</u> of Indian mysticism, as well as the <u>nirvana</u> of Buddhism, strive for the disintegration of one's individuality into a universal bliss. Both are the ultimate end of their religious systems. In other words, the goal of these doctrines is to receive a liberation, and isolation, which means "being like nothing else."[15]

84

In that case, ego would be outside of space and time, and the eternal would be separated in man from the temporal. That is why, as Geoffrey Parrinder says, "The Indian religion has often been described as world-denying, ascetic and selfish retreat from the problems of life."[16] Because of this strict isolation of ego from life, time and space, the Hindu or Buddhist mystic cannot help his followers directly and personally after his death (contrary to the sufi). Why not? "Because," says Toynbee, "since his death, he is in the state of Nirvana (or Moksa); and a being who has made his exit into Nirvana (or Moksa) is deemed to have become inaccessible . . . Nirvana (or Moksa) is a post-personal state of being."[17]

In this respect, nirvana and moksha are to be carefully distinguished from fana, ecstatic mystical union with God in sufism. For one thing, fana is not an end in sufism. It is a means. Liberation or isolation is not the goal of the sufi. Nicholson saw this distinguished characteristic of sufism.

> It is not enough, for a sufi, to escape from all that is creaturely, without entering into the eternal life of God, the Creator as manifested in His works. To abide in God after having passed away from selfhood is the mark of the perfect man (al-Insan al-kamil), who not only journeys to God, but in and with God continuing in the unitive state, he returns with God (as-sayr ani'l-lah bi'l-lah) to the phenomenal world from which he set out and manifests unity in plurality (al-Wahda fi'l-kasra).[18]

The great Turkish mystic poet, Niyazi Misri (16th century) said "To be able find unity in diversity or plurality, is a knowledge which contains and in which are hidden all divine and eternal knowledges."

So matters have not concluded with the attainment of fana. On the contrary, in the sufi undertanding, it is at this point that the real work begins. The sufi, cleansed now by fana, must plunge back into events and existence in the service of others. The Quran says, "Man is God's viceroy in the world."[19]

As God's viceroy, man discovers himself to be in a relationship of indebtedness to this Lord. He is obliged to shape the world within his sphere of influence in a manner most pleasing to his Creator and hence the constant emphasis on activity.

In short, we cannot identify fana with nirvana or moksha. For the latter, the essential point is negation. The former is always accompanied with an abiding in God (baqa) and an activity for the life and mankind. By the way, we must say that it is not credible to maintain a supposition, as Zaehner did that the origin of the concept of fana is Buddhistic-Vedantic. Indeed, "The advocates of Buddhistic or Vedantic origin forget that the main current of Indian influence upon Islamic civilization belongs to a later epoch."[20]

As a conclusion, I turn to one of the most important Sufi thinkers, Kalabadhi (385/995), summing up what he said in his great work concerning fana and baqa.

> Passing away is a state in which all passions pass away . . . Persistence (baqa) which follows passing-away, means that the mystic passes away from what belongs to himself, and passes through what is God's. Persistence is the station of the Prophet . . When a man persists, all things become for him but one thing, and his every motion is in accord with God: He passes away from dissector, and persists in accord . . .[21]

Again, action is the dominant character of Sufism. It is also one of its fundamental principles. The principle might be expressed "It is insufficient to refrain from doing evil." One must actively do good. Reaching nirvana or moksha is attaining to a state in which one becomes passive in respect to evil. For Sufis, there is yet a more exalted state - a more advanced stage. This is a stage beyond mystical union in which one becomes a force of good in the world. "The best of men are those who are useful to others," pronounced the Prophet.[22] He went on to positively forbid any man to turn his back on life in the world. "The believer who participates in human life, exposing himself to its torments and suffering, is worth more than the one who distances himself from its suffering."[23] He said "Human creatures are the families of God and the ones who are most loved by Him, are those who are most useful to His families."

86

Preparation

The education of the sufi takes place along the thorny
highways and byways of life. Membership in a sufi
order has always implied service to man. In fact, the
greater spiritual ascent of a sufi, the more intense
his involvement in human life and the affairs of the
world. As Imam Rabbani, one of the greatest of Islamic
mystics would have put it, "The ascent of a sufi is
proportional to his descent." In other words, the
height of a sufi's rise into the realm of divinity and
spirit is measured by the depth of his descent into
the mundane realm of worldly affairs. Sufism,
therefore, rejects such practices as adhering to
special diets, celibacy and the renunciation of family
life. Muhammad remains the model for the sufi way of
life. He did not live this way and the entire effort
of the sufi is directed toward living as Muhammad
lived.

In short, escape from the world in any of its
myriad forms cannot be a measure of sufi perfection.
The Arabic word captures perfectly the balance
required in sufi life. Baqa means annihilation of the
self in an eternal union with God coupled with a
missionary vocation to mankind. The sufi way entails a
return to the starting point. In the words of my late
teacher, Abdulbaqi Golpinarli, one of the great names
in the annals of sufi historians, on the curve of sufi
ascent there are stages and degrees of fana. However,
those who attain these degrees do not reach maturity.
To rise to maturity, it is necessary to return to the
place from which one began one's sufi training. This
"returning to the beginning" is the phrase employed by
Junayd.

The word farq is used by sufis to designate the
condition of one who has abandoned the things of this
world and becomes entranced in a union with God. This
condition is accepted as a temporary expedient, a
necessary stage in the ascent to self knowledge, but
its prolongation is discouraged. Farq must become jam
and this jam refers to an ecstatic state of mind in
which a consciousness of the unity of God is central.
The ascent to jam, therefore necessarily entails a
return to life and man. In this state, both Creator and
created are viewed together. In the words of the

87

Turkish sufi, Kusadali Ibrahim, <u>jam</u> means "to unite intimacy with God and intimacy with man."[24] Union with God is experienced in a condition of union with His creation. Islamic thought accords minimal value to a God-man union achieved at the cost of abandoning the world for in this there is a denial of the truth of unity.

FOOTNOTES

1. Robert C. Zaehner, Matter and Spirit; NY: Harper & Row, 1963, p. 46.

2. Muhammad Iqbal, Javidnama tr Arthur J. Arberry; Lahore: n.d., p. 21.

3. Arthur J. Arberry, Sufism; NY: Harper & Row, 1970, p. 11.

4. Agehanada Bharati, The Light at the Center; Santa Barbara: Ross-Erickson, 1976, p. 61.

5. Reynold Nicholson, The Mystics of Islam; London: Routledge & Kegan Paul, 1963, pp. 2-3.

6. Evelyn Underhill, Mysticism; London: Methuen, 1912, p. 9.

7. Margaret Smith, The Way of the Mystics; NY: Oxford, 1978 (original 1931), p. 1.

8. Ibid., pp. 4-8.

9. Nicholson, op. cit., pp. 148-149.

10. For these definitions, see Kalabadhi, al-Taarruf, Chapter 1.

11. For the last definition, see Yasar Nuri Ozturk, Kur'an ve Sunnete Gore Tasavvuf (Sufism from the Perspective of the Koran and the Sunna); Istanbul: 1979, pp. 14-18.

12. Nicholson, op. cit., p. 1.

13. Arberry, op. cit., p. 12.

14. The Quran, Sura LV:29.

15. Robert C. Zaehner, Hindu and Muslim Mysticism; NY: Schocken, 1972 (original 1960), p. 39.

16. Arnold Toynbee, The Life After Death; NY: McGraw-Hill, 1976 (original 1960), p. 93.

17. Ibid., p. 11.

18. Nicholson, op. cit., p. 163.

19. Sura II:30.

20. Nicholson, op. cit., p. 9.

21. Kalabadhi, op. cit., Chapter 59.

22. al-Bukhari, riqaq.

23. Ibn Maja, fitan, 23.

24. See, Ozturk, Kusadali Ibrahim ve Tasavvufi Dusunceleri (Kusadali Ibrahim and his Mystic Thoughts); Istanbul: 1982, p. 128.

The Buddhist Outlook on Poverty and Human Rights

Bhikkhu Sunanda Putuwar

The purpose of this article is to examine the secular outlook of Buddhism regarding poverty and human rights. It is true that the main purpose of the Buddha's teaching concerns itself with spiritual liberation. The Buddha, however, did not ignore or exclude secular concerns, including political freedom and economic security. His teaching was offered for the happiness and welfare of the many. He did not believe one group, no matter how privileged or powerful, had the right to dominate others, ruling with the tactics of fear. His compassion concerned each group and each individual. According to Buddhism, no one is superior or inferior by virtue of birth, caste, sex, race, or color. Differences among people are determined by their actions,[1] education and other factors. Economic status is an important factor differentiating one individual or group from others.

Of course, there are various causes for poverty. Causes of poverty are as complex as human society itself. A person can be poor due to various factors: dwelling in a bad or hostile environment, living in an area where natural disasters such as hurricanes occur, living in areas where there is no rain or where there is flooding. Accidents, illness, being robbed or deprived of one's job and having no other resources-all contribute to poverty.

Some people do not have sufficient energy to work productively when hunger is a constant factor. Others lose all hope for the future and are sunk in despair, without realizing their lot could be improved. There are many psychological, political, social, and economic factors which contribute to individual and national poverty. One of the causes of poverty depicted in the early Buddhist texts is that caused by the inadequate or corrupt political administration of a nation. Various calamities will erupt when the ruler of the

91

country is immoral or corrupt and administration is poor. Calamities such as hunger or famine, disease and dangers of various kinds will occur. Rahula said that "He (the Buddha) had shown how a whole country could become corrupt, degenerate and unhappy when the heads of its government, that is, the king, the ministers and administrative officers become corrupt and unjust."[2]

Another cause of poverty is an individual's personal addiction to vice. This state of affairs not only destroys one's own wealth, but, indirectly may cause the destruction of the economy as a whole. A Buddhist scripture says that the cause of poverty is addiction to women, wine, and intoxicating drugs. Dice (gambling) or spending all that has been acquired is the cause of one's ruin. On a personal level, overindulgence in sleep, pursuing a licentious life, talking too much, not being energetic and becoming easily angry all may cause ruin.[3]

Illiteracy, the misuse of funds, bad associations with friends, and disease all contribute to loss. Whatever the cause, poverty is painful. The Buddha rightly said that to be without what one needs (desires) is painful.[4] I would like to offer my own experience of poverty in Nepal as an example for you to consider.

A farmer with average skills in the rural areas of Nepal earns hardly half dollar a day.[5] They do not have nutritious food. They do not have coats and boots or any other sufficient clothing for the cold season. They cannot even imagine a heating system or indoor bathrooms. Most houses are poorly built. In rural areas most houses are thatched, built in one or two stories. Many of us do not have any shelter, except for a lean-to. We have to drink muddy water when it rains. We have life-threatening diseases such as tuberculosis, chronic diarrhea and-other diseases. Most places have no hospitals with trained doctors and adequate medical facilities. As a consequence, we die from even simple causes. About 80% of the population is illiterate. We have a high birth rate. The majority of Nepalese people have never seen a telephone nor television. The possession of a watch or a radio is regarded as a sign of wealth. Only about 23% of our land is arable. Without the co-operation of rich and powerful nations it will be very difficult for us to overcome this tragic poverty.

Inequalities amongst human beings, according to the Buddha, occur because of varying conditions. Yet the sun, air, water, and empty space are regarded as the common property of all. Everyone has a right to enjoy and live with their benefits. Everyone has a right to eat, drink, work, and to be educated, and to live in peace and security. The world's major problems, therefore, are concerned with economic imbalances. World population steadily increases, but there is no increase of resource to maintain ourselves. Unless powerful nations of people co-operate, or rather assist the needy, the words, "human rights" will only remain a beautiful sound like "a love song without the lover."

To overcome this tragic situation and actualize human rights we must act individually and collectively. The poor are the helpless. We should see all human beings as equally human beings. By comparing other beings with oneself, one should learn not to strike or kill others.[6]

In Southern Buddhism, there is no principle which states that an external force will bestow awards or punishments. Rather it is our own actions which determine the outcome of any act of body, speech, or mind. Therefore, one acts and receives the consequences of one's actions. We must trust ourselves in our own ability to make or destroy the world. The Buddha said, "By effort one overcomes suffering."[7]

Buddhist ethics extol energetic effort in all areas. Men or women should act on their own behalf and do benevolent things for others as well. One who does not work can be considered as a burden to society, consuming things which others have acquired. To live is to act. The Buddha said, "Better is a life of a single day for one who strenuously makes effort than that one should live a hundred years idle and inactive."[8] The Buddha, addressing the monks, pointed out the disadvantages of being lazy. If a shopkeeper is lazy - one who at early dawn attends not closely to his work, nor yet at midday, nor again at eventide then he can hardly acquire more property which he has not yet earned, nor can he protect property which he has already earned, nor can he increase what he presently possesses.[9] If workers choose a livelihood suitable to their natures, then if the work is

93

profitable and if they attend their duties punctually and are industrious in their effort, they will earn money.[10]

It is true that a lazy person can hardly acquire wealth in comparison to one who is not lazy. Laziness blocks further earnings which have not yet been earned. A lazy person can also dissipate property which one has already possessed. The lazy person who does not work, or do what he or she ought to do makes excuses, thinking, "It is very cold, extremely hot; it is too early, it is too late; I am now very hungry and thirsty, or now my stomach is too full because I have just eaten."[11] The indolent person thinks in these ways and does not work. It stands to reason that if one does not work then one will not acquire economic security.

Here the Buddha tried to encourage people to pay attention to earning wealth in a correct manner. He said that men who have not acquired wealth in youth, pine away like old herons in a pond from which fish have disappeared. One reminiscences and regrets lost opportunities.[12]

Some people misinterpret the Buddha's teaching as completely other worldly. This is absolutely incorrect. The Buddha's advice concerning worldly possessions is only a warning on not clinging too much to possessions. If you are too attached to worldly possessions, even to your own family and your own body, you are liable to face dissatisfaction, pain, and frustration from the inevitable change. In fact, the Buddha shows the importance of leading a wholesome worldly life. He encourages and advises the laity to earn and accumulate wealth in a manner befitting and moral.

The Buddha said the wealth worth having in the present state of life consists of four parts.[13] Let us consider them one by one. They are:

1. Utthanasampada. To possess energy and skill in whatever work is undertaken and to be diligent in duty concerned with one's work as right livelihood. One should try by all correct means to increase secular possession or property.

2. Arakkhasampada. Not only should one earn and

94

accumulate (amass) property in a correct manner, one should also take good care to maintain it so that it will not be ruined or spoiled. If a person loans property to anyone he ought not ignore it, but retrieve it in due course of time. In more practical matters of everyday life, an ancient precept advises the lending of valuable items only to persons who will respect the principle of caring for such articles in their temporary ownership, returning them as agreed upon. On the other hand, one can freely offer certain items to close relatives, needy neighbors or poor persons without expectation of their return. One should not, however, be carelessly ensnared by flattery.

3. Kalyanamittata. One should cultivate good friends and maintain friendship, win good-hearted comrades and associates. Such friendships are mutually beneficial and help protect one's health, wealth, name, and fame.

4. Samajivikata. One should live in proportion to one's income. Extravagance or stinginess are two extremes which should be avoided.

A family's possessions can be dissipated in four ways: they do not seek what is lost, they do not replace things worn out, they do not know moderation in spending, they put in authority a man or woman who is immoral.[14]

According to the Buddha, possessing wealth has five benefits for householders. They are as follow: (1) a householder can feed parents, wife, children, and employees so they will live happily, (2) friends can be helped, (3) dangers can be warded off, (4) contributions can be made to relatives and ancestors, guests can be welcomed, government duties and taxes can be paid, and (5) religious offerings can be made.[15] Thus it is useful and necessary for a person to have possessions. According to the Buddha, a householder has various sorts of happiness derived from conditions of economic security such as, happiness from having sufficient wealth; happiness in liberally spending the wealth for himself, for his family, relatives, and friends; and happiness from being free from debt.[16]

According to the Buddha, a person should divide his income into four portions: one portion of the whole

95

covers home expenses such as food, clothing, housing, and medical care in daily life; two portion are used as capital for running a business; and the last one portion is to be saved for emergencies. Such a householder can live confidently and happily.[17]

The lack of necessary maintenance undermines the dignity of human beings and distorts the meaning of the human family and the life of a nation. However, we should be optimistic that we may be able to overcome this tragic situation. The poor must be taught and supported to aspire to a higher quality of life by educating them to realize their rights in society. They must try to overcome poverty.

The Buddha encourage "haves" to assist or give (caga) to "have-nots," without expecting anything in return. When the "have-nots" do not receive assistance, stealing with occur and when stealing spreads, then violence, killing, murder, corruption, abusive speech, covetousness and all kinds of immoral actions will occur.[18] The Buddha does not teach "have-nots" to be jealous of "haves," nor does he force "haves" to give to "have-nots." He knew that when force must be used, society cannot be peaceful. Force has no permanent value for global peace. According to the Buddha, although the government may suppress such situations by punishment, such punishment alone will not alleviate the causative factors. Government has to improve the economic conditions of the country by providing jobs, proper wages, capital and other assistance to remove poverty.[19] Number one of the "Ten Duties of the King" is liberality, generosity, charity (dana). The ruler should not crave and be attached to wealth and property, but should give it away for the welfare of the people."[20] The ruler should practice non-violence, try to promote peace and prevent war.

It is easy for powerful nations to help friendly nations. The poor and the disenfranchised do not need any nuclear missiles or any other ammunition. What the poor want is something to eat. If we could minimize or do away with greed, hatred and delusion, it would not be necessary to manufacture weapons, ammunition, and so on, spending billions of dollars and keeping the world's population on the edge of destruction.

How much greater life would be if instead of being directed by anger and delusion and spending so much

96

money and using so many resources for the purpose of destroying others, we shared with others. In this way, we would be able to strengthen love, gain peace and make social progress rather than continually developing and sustaining animosity. Consider how practical the Buddha's teaching is. He said, "He who gives wins friends."[21] We all like peace, but we all prepare for war. How can we change our world with such motifs? First of all we must change our mind before we can change the world situation. Each of us must start with himself or herself first if we desire to move towards towards our global goal. We make the world we want.

1. Dines Andersen and Helmer Smith, eds., Sutta-Nipata; London: Luzac, 1965, p. 23.

2. Walpola Rahula, What The Buddha Taught; NY: Grove, 1959, p. 84.

3. Sutta-Nipata, op. cit., p. 19.

4. Herman Oldenberg, ed., The Vinaya Pitakam (The Mahavagga), Vol. 1; London: Luzac, 1964, p.10.

5. Central Bureau of Statistics; Kathmandu: His Majesty's Government of Nepal, 1985.

6. The Dhammapada, Pali Text and Translation with Stories in Brief and Notes by Narada Thera; Colombo: Vajirarama, 2515-1972, 10:1.

7. M. Leon Feer, ed., The Samyutta-Nikaya of the Sutta-Pitaka, part 1; London: Luzac, 1960, p. 214.

8. The Dhammapada 8:13.

9. F.L. Woodward, tr., The Book of the Gradual Sayings (Anguttara-Nikaya), Vol. 1; London: Luzac, 1960, p. 99.

10. The Samyutta-Nikaya of the Sutta Pitaka, Part 1, p. 214.

11. T.W. and C.A.F. Rhys Davids, trs., Dialogues of the Buddha (The Digha-Nikaya), part 111; London: Luzac, 1965, p. 176.

12. See The Dhammapada 12: 10-11.

13. E. Hardy, ed., The Anguttara-Nikaya Vol. IV; London: Luzac, 1958, pp. 285-287.

14. F.L. Woodward, tr., The Book of the Gradual Sayings (Anguttara-Nikaya). Vol. 11; London: Luzac, 1962, pp. 254-255.

15. E. Hardy, ed., The Anguttara-Nikaya, part 111; London: Luzac, 1958, pp. 45-46.

16. Rahula, op. cit., p. 83.

17. Dialogues of the Buddha (Digha-Nikaya), Part 111, p. 180.

18. Ibid., Part 111, p. 65f.

19. T.W. Rhys David, tr., Dialogues of the Buddha, Part 1; London: Luzac, 1956, pp. 175-176.

20. Rahula, op. cit., p. 85

21. The Samyutta-Nikaya of the Sutta-Pitaka, Part 1, p. 215.

BIBLICAL WISDOM

Henry O. Thompson

It is a pleasure to dedicate this essay to Dr. Sebastian Alexander Matzcak on the occasion of his 75th birthday. He has worked long and hard in the Lord's vineyard on philosophy which means "the love of wisdom." Thus it seems appropriate to write about the Lord's book and the love of wisdom there. The Wise women and men, the sages of ancient Israel, were the teachers of their people. Dr. Matczak's wisdom, knowledge, understanding, insight, perception - garnered over a life time of teaching - puts him squarely in the great tradition of the wisdom movement and the biblical tradition.

Introduction

The Hebrew Bible is divided into three parts - Torah [law or instruction; Greek Pentateuch], Nebiim [prophets] and Kethubim [writings]. Sometimes it is called the TaNaK or Tanakh from the initial letters of the three parts. The Wisdom tradition is usually associated with the Writings, in such books as Proverbs, Job, Ecclesiates or Qoheleth, Ecclesiasticus or Ben Sirach and the Wisdom of Solomon.[1]

The Hebrew word for "wisdom" is "chokmah" or "hokmah." It is found 147 times in the Hebrew Scriptures while a variant noun form "hokmoth" occurs four times. The adjective "hakam," "wise," occurs 135 times while the verb, "hakam," is found 26 times. The other half of the occurrences of the noun and verb are in Proverbs, Job and Ecclesiastes. Wisdom in the Bible is not limited to the actual word. There are several terms used with or as synonyms for wisdom including several derivatives of "bin," "perceive" such as "nabon," "perceptive," "skillful," (Gen 41:33, etc.), "binah," "insight," (Dt 4:6, etc.), "tebunah," "insight," "skill" of a worker (Ex 36:1, etc.).

101

Several forms of "yada'," "to know," (Jer 4:22, etc.), including "da'at," "knowledge" (Pr 5:2, etc.) emphasize understanding (Job 34:2), experience (Dt 1:13), art and magic (Is 47:10). The heart, "leb," in Hebrew is associated with thought and wisdom (Job 9:4; I Kings 10:24), including skill and ability (Ex 28:3, etc). All of this was expressed in proverbs, riddles, allegories, hymns, dialogues, autobiography, lists of nouns (animals, plants, etc.) and didactic narrative, both poetry and prose.[2]

The Writings and Beyond

Wisdom material is not limited to the official wisdom books. It is found elsewhere, including other portions of the Writings such as some of the psalms, e.g., 1, 32, 34, 37, 49, 112, 128. The book of Esther is attributed to a sage who shows how wisdom and integrity bring rewards. The book of Daniel shows him as a wise man who interpreted dreams and spirit writing on the wall in the court of the Babylonian King Nebuchadnezzar. Daniel may have been an historical figure in the 500s B.C. though modern scholarship dates the writing to 168-5 B.C., the time of the Hasmonean or Maccabean revolt. Earlier, Ezekiel, a prophet in Babylon in the time of Nebuchadnezzar (605-562 B.C.), referred to Daniel along with Noah and Job (14:14, 20) as righteous and as a sage (Ezek 28:3). There was a wise king name Dan'el in the ancient Ugaritic literature, dated c. 1400 B.C. Some consider both the book of Daniel and Ezekiel's reference to be to this Ugaritic king who "judged" (cared for) the widow and the orphan.[3]

Earlier, the Joseph stories in Genesis have been called wisdom writing. Joseph was the wise courtier interpreting dreams and giving counsel to the pharaoh. The whole of Gen 1-11 has been called wisdom material. The story of the fall includes a tree of knowledge and the knowledge of good and evil (Gen 3). This is part of the so-called Yahwist or "J" narrative that is part of the Pentateuch from Gen 2:4b through Numbers. All of J has been called wisdom writing. Moses and Aaron (Ex 7:8- 13) performed miracles. The wise men of Egypt did also but God prevailed (8:18-19). This is part of the so-called Priestly or "P" narrative intertwined in the Pentateuch from Gen 1:1 through Numbers. The court history of David in II Sam 9-20 and I Kings 1-2 has been related to wisdom writing. The wise woman from Tekoa (II Sam 14:1-24) helped General Joab solve a problem for King David. David himself is proclaimed as having wisdom (vs 20).[4]

Isaiah has been called a sage or at least he used wisdom language.

> For to us a child is born, to us a son is given;
> and the government will be upon his shoulder,
> and his name will be called
> "Wonderful Counselor, Mighty God,
> Everlasting Father, Prince of Peace. (9:6)

> And the Spirit of the Lord shall rest upon him,
> the spirit of wisdom and understanding,
> the spirit of counsel and might,
> the spirit of knowledge and the fear of the LORD.
> (11:2)

> ..the earth will be full of the knowledge of the
> LORD.. (11:9)

There is an analogy with a farmer, instructed by God in 28:23-29. God is described as wise in 31:2.

This continues in the second part of the book, commonly called II Isaiah where God

> frustrates the omens of liars,
> and makes fools of diviners;
> .. turns wise men back
> and makes their knowledge foolish
> ..confirms the word of his servant,
> and performs the counsel of his messengers.
> (Is 44:25-26)

Sheldon Blank suggested this continues the court tradition of Joseph, Moses and Aaron, and Daniel, all of whom also triumphed over the "locals." Is 40:6-7 is a wisdom riddle; 59:4-6 uses language from nature to describe the wicked. Amos, Hosea, Jeremiah, Habakkuk, Micah and Jonah have also been cited for their affinity with wisdom. Amos, for example, shared the ethics of the wisdom movement with his concern for loving the good, practicing justice, hating evil. Habakkuk raised a philosophical type of question about divine justice.

103

These prophetic observations could, of course, be reversed. Instead of the prophets using wisdom language and motifs, it may have been the sages who were using prophetic language. We could include here the so-called Deuteronomic theology - be good and you will be blessed. Be bad and you will be punished. While there is much truth in this, the real world often seems quite unjust where evil is rewarded and goodness punished. Out of this came the question of theodicy - the problem of evil - and such books as Job. Here we simply note that the thought of ancient Israel was divided into distinct genres such as prophecy and wisdom, but the distinction should not be drawn so sharply as to suggest there was no relationship among them.[5]

Solomon: Patron of Wisdom

The clearest "elsewhere" of wisdom beyond the official wisdom books in the Bible is in the stories of King Solomon. Solomon is the patron saint or founding father or eponymous ancestor of the biblical wisdom tradition. The materials in I Kings include his prayer for an understanding mind (3:9) and his wise judgement (3:16-28) as well as the tradition of his 1005 songs and 3000 proverbs (4:32). In II Chronicles 1:10, Solomon prayed for "wisdom and knowledge."[6]

His "wise judgement" is what today we might call common sense or insight in human nature. The story in I Kings 3 is about two women who both claimed a child. Solomon said cut the kid in two and give each woman half. One said fine and the other said, "No. Let the child live. The other woman can have it." Solomon realized, of course, that this was the real mother.

According to I Kings 10, the Queen of Sheba came to test his wisdom. In the apocryphal literature, there is a story about one of these tests. She had two roses - one real, and one so skillfully made that the human eye could not tell the difference. She put the two at the far end of the throne room and challenged Solomon to tell which one was real. He asked for time for such a difficult task, and used the time to send an assistant out to catch a bee which was released in the room, and of course went to the real rose.[7]

Solomon is the traditional author of Proverbs,

Job, Qoheleth and the Wisdom of Solomon though modern scholarship dates the writing of these to the post-Exilic period.[8] It is of interest that the Writings (Greek, "Hagiographa") section of the Tenak was not officially canonized or officially accepted as scripture until the Council of Jabneh/Jamnia c. 90 A.D.[9] Other references (Luke 24:44) suggestion that portions of them, such as the psalms, were already accepted as scripture and that probably includes the material most strongly related to Solomon, though questions remained about the Song of Songs. Modern scholarship recognizes the possibility that some of the material, such as portions of Proverbs, might indeed go back to Solomon though we do not know that for sure. There is also the recognition that the written form has an oral tradition behind it. While the current form of the material may have been written at a later date, the tradition itself may go back to a much earlier time.[10]

The Ancient Near East

The view of an "earlier time" has been enhanced by the discovery of wisdom material throughout the Near or Middle East, and indeed throughout the world.[11] For centuries, the Western world knew the Bible in isolation. It had survived the past without a context. Some other ancient writings had also survived, such as Plato and related works. Others came to lighten the dark ages via the Muslims and Jews of Spain. The Crusades brought renewed contacts between the East and Europe. The fall of Constantinople in 1453 brought a small flood of Greek manuscripts and Greek scholars to the West.

However, it was not until more recent travellers, explorers and archaeologists began to bring the Eastern "light" to the benighted West that the full context of the Bible began to appear. Travellers such as Pietro della Valle (1616) and Athanasius Kircher (1643) published copies of Mesopotamian cuneiform and Egyptian hieroglyphics with more coming to light with the spade. Gradually the ancient languages were translated and the mind of the ancients was open to the modern world. The Bible no longer stuck up out of the past like a lone pyramid. The biblical bit is more like the tip of an iceberg with only the top showing. The far greater amount of the past was hidden out of sight. In recent generations, this past has been exposed by artist and archaeologist. Temples and palaces, houses and bones do not tell us much about the wisdom tradition but the ancient writings do.[12]

Among the myths and legends, the poetry and the unending records of administration, there are wisdom writings inscribed on temple walls, stelae, Mesopotamian clay tablets and Egyptian papyrii. These date back to the Pyramid Age of Egypt (2600-2400 B.C.) and among the Sumerians (3000-1900) in Mesopotamia. But these dated writings are based on an earlier oral tradition. Indeed, given the nature of the wisdom tradition, one suspects it goes back to the dawn of time and is part and parcel of the "human" as distinguished from the animal. Some find animal life exhibiting a good bit of wisdom as well.

Unity in Diversity

Bernhard W. Anderson and others note two types of wisdom material. One is practical advice, especially to the young on how to achieve happiness and a good life. Here we find the biblical book of Proverbs, the Egyptian "Teaching of Amen-em-opet," "The Instruction of Ptahhotep" and the Egyptian "Counsels of Wisdom." The practical side of wisdom continues unabated today, at times in a veritable flood of self-help books, the power of positive thinking of Norman Vincent Peale and Robert Schuler's possibility thinking, and popular journals like Psychology Today.[13]

Walter Harrelson pointed out the universal and contemporaneous nature of wisdom. He cited Benjamin Franklin from an earlier day. Dale Carnegie, Amy Vanderbilt, Ann Landers and Art Buchwald are examples today of this type of wisdom. Crenshaw cites as wisdom's heritage its ability to cope with reality and one could find that here in these examples of practical help. Psychotherapists are the now version of the wise women and men of the past. Counselors do not stay in the psychological domain, however, for they are found in the halls of government, business and academe. It is no accident that lawyers are often called "counselors." In religion, many sermons have been preached in a tradition sometimes called moralizing. We find them in Judaism, Christianity, Islam, Buddhism and others. The teachings of Confucius are an outstanding

106

example to which one could add the teachings of countless gurus (teachers) in Hinduism, Sikhism, Jainism, Shinto and Zen.[14]

The second type of wisdom is a reflection on life and its meaning such as Job and Ecclesiates in the Bible, the Egyptian "Dispute over Suicide" and the Babylonian "I will Praise the Lord of Wisdom" (the Lord is the god Marduk). Anderson sees here wisdom as the fundamental human concern. "The quest for wisdom is the quest for the meaning of life."[15]

Here again modern psychology has been on the forefront of a continuing effort. One could note Abraham Maslow's hierarchy of needs - survival, achievement, recognition and the peak experience, along with other humanistic psychologies. Out of the concentration camps of Nazi Europe came the observation the people can withstand incredible trauma when they have a purpose for living, a sense of meaning in life. Victor Frankl's logotherapy opened new vistas for human understanding.[16]

Traditional religion has offered humanity meaning and purpose for many centuries. The range is enormous. Augustine's famous prayer noted that "our hearts are restless, O Lord, until they find their rest in thee." The Hebrew prophets reached sublime heights as in Micah 6:8, "What doth the Lord require of thee but to do justice, to love mercy and to walk humbly with thy God?" Much of Christian history has been concerned with salvation and getting to heaven but there are echoes of alternatives. Jesus said, "Not all who say 'Lord! Lord!' shall enter the kingdom of heaven but the one that does the will of my heavenly father" (Mt 7:21). On occasion, some have objected to an exclusive focus on heaven with the aphorism, "Some folks are so heavenly minded, they are no earthly good." For this world, Gautama the Buddha advised that all is suffering but this can be relieved by giving up all desire (some say give up "selfish" desire). A more positive view of life's meaning is in terms of the religious tradition to love - God, neighbor, self - found in all the major religions and many minor ones as well.[17] Along with the Golden or Silver Rule, love is about as close to a universal ethic as we have. Thus it might be said to combine practical wisdom with the meaningful life wisdom.

Perhaps the pursuit of meaning is even more obvious in philosophy - the love of wisdom. The biblical prophet Habakkuk who asked "How long, O Lord, how long?" in 605 B.C. The Athenian philosopher Socrates responded to the practical question, "Are we good by nature or nurture?" He asked in return, "What is good?" Throughout the ages, philosophers have asked the probing questions. They have developed elaborate schemes filling many volumes without coming to an acceptable conclusion. Many, such as the existentialists, have fallen into despair with skepticism about finding an answer. The Danish Christian Soren Kierkegaard and the Germanic Friedrich Nietzsche and the French atheist Jean Paul Sartre faced the "meaninglessness" of life.

But this is not new to modern critical depressions. The psalmist (22:1) cried out, "My God, my God! Why hast thou forsaken me?" One could hear pessimism in, "What is man that thou art mindful of him?" (8:4) Qoheleth the preacher noted that "vanity, all is vanity." There is, however, in the biblical tradition of the quest for meaning, a great "tour de force" sometimes called the great "nevertheless." We see it starkly put in Job, "Though he slay me, nevertheless I will yet worship him." Ps 8 proceeds quickly from the insignificance of man to the next breath, "and yet, thou hast made him but little lower than the angels and dost crown him with glory and honor" (vs 5). The Preacher ends with the end of the matter: "Fear God, and keep his commandments for this is the whole duty of man." Or, as Proverbs records it, "The fear of the Lord is the beginning of wisdom" (9:10).[18]

Divine and Human

This last phrase is background for two dimensions or aspects of the practical and the meaningful wisdom that sometimes get divorced. Much of the wisdom literature, both in the Bible and in the rest of the ancient Near East, has been called secular, humanistic. It applies to humanity without regard to their ethnic origins or group. There is nothing specifically Hebraic in

A living dog is better than a dead lion (Ecc 9:4).

Or,

A wise son makes a glad father,

but a foolish son is a sorrow to his mother
(Pr 10:1).

Such wisdom, like the aphorisms that appear on modern
calendars, in otherwise unused space in magazines or
newspapers, the famous bits in Reader's Digest, is
often common to all humanity. This has led some to call
this kind of wisdom, secular, i.e., not spiritual, not
religious. Secondarily, it has led to the opinion that
the wisdom tradition does not fit with the rest of
biblical tradition, i.e., a tradition defined "a
priori" without considering the wisdom material.[19]

This is modern "eisegesis," "reading into" the
text a modern split or bifurcation that did not exist
in ancient time and indeed is a relatively modern
perspective. Some religious traditions even yet today
believe that all of life is sacred. There is no
secular. God is concerned with all of life. The
spiritual is a dimension of all life. The limitation of
religion to one hour of the week on the sabbath,
leaving the rest of the week secular, is a recent
innovation in the West. Part of the attraction of
eastern traditions in western culture may very well be
the continuing wholeness and continuity of life which
recognizes the spiritual or sacral character of all
existence - human, animal, plant, mineral - "the rocks
and rills and templed hills" are all part of the
divine domain.[20]

Part of that wholeness is the unity of the
feminine and the masculine dimensions of existence,
including God. God created people - female and male -
in God's image. That ought to mean God is both though
God in the Hebrew-Christian-Muslim tradition is
normally referred to as "he," perhaps in opposition to
ancient fertility cults, perhaps as male chauvinism on
the part of males who preserved the records. The
wisdom movement was a creature of its time, in many
ways, including this one. But we note some exceptions,
not least of which is that Wisdom herself is presented
as a woman. The Hebrew "chokmah" is a feminine noun.
Pr 8 presents wisdom as a personified feminine
dimension of God. The Egyptian Ma'at - symbol of
knowledge, truth, the order of the cosmos - is a

goddess.[21]

The number of wise women listed is rather limited.
The most well known of these is the wise woman of
Tekoa whom Joab brought to King David to help him
solve the problem of his son Absolom (II Sam 14). There
are many references to virtuous and evil women. The
chauvinism of the latter is the presentation of the
woman as tempter without due regard to male
responsibility not only for sexual sin but for all
other types as well. The reference in Pr 10:1 to both
fathers and mothers was cited earlier. Mothers do not
appear often in the wisdom literature but there are
several examples. Pr 31:1-9 are the words of Lemuel
which his mother taught him. Pr 31:10-31 describes a
good wife. "Her children rise up and call her blessed"
(vs 28). The Egyptian "Instruction of Ani" includes a
paragraph reminding the son to remember his mother who
carried him in her womb and breast fed him for three
years.[22]

All of life is sacred. There is no secular. What
is more, wisdom was the gift of God or the gods in a
polytheistic tradition. In the Hebrew tradition, only
God has access to wisdom. Even in a non-theistic
tradition, it is part of the sacredness of life. In
this regard, wisdom is every bit as much at home in
the Bible as the Torah and the Dabar (word; Greek
"logos"). God gave the Torah - law or instruction - to
Moses on Mt. Sinai. Modern scholarship notes that this
frame of reference is contrived. Many of the laws can
be found in other traditions.[23]

The Law Code of Hammurabi dates from c. 1700 B.C.
It was carved on a stone (diorite) slab - a stela -
which was found in Susa where it was probably carried
by the Elamites after a raid on ancient Babylon. On top
of the stela, above the law code carved in cuneiform,
there is a picture of Hammurabi before Shamash the sun
god. Pritchard interprets the relief as Shamash
commissioning Hammurabi to write the code. The law, as
a sacred gift, was common to other traditions.[24]

The Mosaic authorship (or mediatorship) of the law
can be seen as a kind of Constitution. Very few of the
laws of the United States can be found in the
Constitution. But to be valid, legal laws, they must
all be in agreement or in tune with that document. If
it is not, a court or the Supreme Court rules the law

unconstitutional. Laws, even when borrowed from Israel's neighbors, were the gift of God. Wisdom, even when literary form or content can be found paralleled in other lands, was a gift of God. The wisdom with which Solomon judged or with which his or later counselors counseled, was a gift of God. "The people saw that the Lord was with him" (I Kings 3:28).

Today, a counselor might be lawyer. More commonly we think of counseling as therapy. A therapist might go to school and get a Ph.D. or certificate, and hang out a shingle advertising for customers. But if that therapist is a practicing Jew, Christian, Shinto, Buddhist, etc., s/he might very well pray for wisdom to counsel those who come. While much of modern therapy is considered non-religious, i.e., secular, both by practitioners and by counselees, and by the rest of society, there are some who even yet consider it one of the talents that God gives. As such, it is a talent to be used humbly and "wisely" for the benefit of others rather than self-glory. In this sense, Solomon's prayer - not for his own sake but for others - is a prototype of the religionist today who is also a counselor.

It is not unusual for a counselor to help a person in need with practical advice, as well as to help that person find old or new or deeper meaning in life. Both the practical and meaningful forms of wisdom belong to this sacred tradition, which is the gift of God. While it might seem far removed from some direct revelation from on high, it is no more removed than sitting at a table and saying grace for a meal which has moved from farmer's field through processing to grocery stores to baking or cooking before landing on the table. If all of life is under God, than all of these processes are part of his divine providence. One can thank God for dry pavement and sunshine while traveling even though the pavement was built by a contractor and one can thank God for the knowledge to be a lawyer, a therapist or a teacher, even though the books were written and printed by human beings.

The words, of course, are human words. That was true for the biblical prophets as well. But the "dabar," the "word" which they had was from the Lord. They did not preach their own message. It was rather, "Thus says the LORD!" They spoke in Hebrew. In Japan they would have spoken Japanese. In an English

111

speaking area, the Word would have been in English. Or, it might be translated into the human language of the land. But while the words were and are human and are common to what today we call the "secular" world, they were nonetheless believed to be a gift from God. Alternatively, we could say the essence of the message came from God to the prophets who put that "essence" into human words. In the process, the prophets used words, phrases, sayings (including wise sayings) found elsewhere, just as a preacher today draws on a variety of sources for a sermon yet claims to be preaching "the Word of God." Both Jeremiah 31:29 and Ezekiel 18:2, for example, use the traditional, "The fathers have eaten sour grapes and the children's teeth are set on edge."

Jeremiah 18:18 is a key text for our understanding. Some people thought Jeremiah had committed treason in telling the Israelites to accept the Babylonians as instruments of God. They plotted against Jeremiah. Since he was a prophet, there was some danger in this. God might retaliate. But others reassured the colleagues. Not to worry. The law will not perish from the priest, nor counsel ("'esah") from the wise, nor the word from the prophet. All three - law, counsel, word - are seen as gifts from God.

The "counsel" or the words of the wise might very well draw on the language of the day, the wisdom of other cultures, the creation of the wise person's own mind. Discernment itself was a gift of God, whether in the area of practical advice or searching for the meaning of life. And as biblical wisdom was often equated with skill of any kind, so today we might say that all human talents - whether singing or carpentry, writing or prayer, art or business management - are gifts of God. Wisdom was not secular in its context. There was no secular. All of life was sacred. It was and is humanistic but not humanistic in the non-theistic way that term is often used today. "The fool has said in his heart there is no God (Ps 14:1)."

The Teacher

Several references already cited refer to teaching. The concept of teacher or learning is not limited to the wisdom material. The Hebrew "torah," commonly

112

translated "law," is often translated as "instruction." The prophets were, of course, teaching their people the will of God in sharing the "Word." And these official leaders were not alone.

Hear, my son, your father's instruction,
and reject not your mother's teaching; (Pr 1:8)

The words of Lemuel.. his mother taught him:
What, my son? What son of my womb? (Pr 31:1-2)

..ask your father and he will show you;
your elders and they will tell you. (Dt 32:7)

Wisdom is with the aged,
and understanding in length of days. (Job 12:12)

But the sages were above all, the teachers. "The sages of Israel" can rightly be phrased, "The teachers of Israel." The Book of Proverbs opens with "The proverbs of Solomon." Then there is an unspoken "Why?" was this collection made?

That men may know wisdom and instruction,
understanding words of insight,
receive instruction in wise dealing,
righteousness, justice, and equity;
that prudence may be given to the simple,
knowledge and discretion to the youth --
the wise man also may hear and increase in learning,
and the man of understanding acquire skill,
to understand a proverb and a figure,
the words of the wise and their riddles. (1:2-7)[25]

Pr. 13:14 claims the teaching of the wise is the fountain of life. They accumulated the knowledge of nature and drew morals and lessons for behavior from the natural world. Later, this type of teaching is called natural revelation and natural law. For theists it is part of the general revelation of God as compared with the specific revelation such as that given to the prophets. For both theists and non-theists, the natural law often provides a basis for ethics. Rylaarsdam noted that at one time, "natural and revealed religion were indistinguishable..."[26]

Teaching the Past

In general, one might say teachers have a responsibility to preserve the knowledge of the past. One could see the wisdom literature - the accumulation of proverbs, riddles, etc. - as the part of this preservation. It is of interest that the sages of Israel were not narrow sectarians in this regard. The entire book of Job is sometimes seen as referring to a non-Israelite, possibly an Edomite. The sayings of Agur (Pr 30:1-4) and Lemuel (31:1-9) are probably of foreign origin. There is some agreement that Pr 22:17-24:22 is borrowed from the Egyptian "Instruction of Amen-em-opet." One need only compare, for example,

> Make no friendship with a man given to anger
> nor go with a wrathful. (Pr 22:24)

> Do not associate to thyself the heated man
> nor visit him for conversation. (Amen-em-Opet
> 11:13-14)

Ultra-conservatives today sometimes condemn any source of knowledge from outside the Bible, or outside the country, without realizing that the biblical writers themselves were borrowing from other cultures. One could say that Truth is of God wherever the Truth is found. Mahatma Gandhi went so far as to say Truth is God and God is Truth.[27]

Teaching the Future

Teachers not only accumulate knowledge of the past. They create new knowledge or at least add to old knowledge through their research. The Preacher said

> I applied my mind to seek and to search out by
> wisdom all that is done under heaven... (Ecc
> 1:13)

In our own day, we have a knowledge explosion. Knowledge is no longer just a matter of adding a little more to what we have. It is increasing additionally but multiplying exponentially or geometrically. Some have suggested we call a halt to all research until we have digested what we already know.

In health care, for example, new procedures have outstripped our moral or ethical ability to handle it. Once, life and death were relatively simple. Now a body can be kept "alive" - heart and lungs pumped by machines - when by natural law, it would be dead. So are these resuscitated corpses or are they persons? If they are corpses, some say we should "pull the plug" and bury the dead body. The sages of today have suggestions here but they do not all agree and many hesitate to pull the plug lest they be charged with murder - and a few have been.[28]

But research goes on. Sometimes this is because of the great rewards of recognition, status, power, and enormous amounts of money - government, foundations, hundreds of groups like The March of Dimes, individuals - that come to the successful researcher. But sometimes, the knowledge is sought for its own sake. For still others, the search for knowledge is their service to God. While both teaching and research today have been secularized to a major extent, those who continue to believe in God will recognize on occasion that all wisdom comes from the LORD. "The fear of the Lord is the beginning of wisdom." Or in the old monastic tradition, "To work is to pray." The researcher's work is a form of prayer, an offering to God.

Teacher as Parent

One could argue that parents are often in the position of the sages in relation to their children, at least when the children are young. The parental responsibility is to teach their children morality and faith, so they can grow up and take their adult responsibilities in an adult world. When they grow up, the children should be able to think for themselves. That may, on occasion, result in disagreement with the parents. Sometimes children get a "disease" known as "sophomoritis" (with apologies to all normal sophomores). They think they know it all. Qoheleth comes close to this when he says "I have seen everything...., all is vanity... (Ecc 1:14).

One could suggest by analogy that God, as a heavenly Father, also wants his children to grow up. Some traditions speak of people as having "free will." That includes freedom to think and even to disagree with their heavenly Father. But the sages knew (1) that they did not know it all, and, (2) the fear of the Lord is the beginning of wisdom. An Iowa cartoonist caught the dilemma in three panels which were published annually on Father's Day for many years. "Ding" Darling showed a child looking up at big Dad. The middle panel showed a gangling teen looking down at little Dad. The third panel showed a mature adult looking at an equal sized Dad. It has been suggested that God calls us to be servants but then we rise from servanthood to being children of God. Ultimately, we become friends of God, like Abraham (II Chr 20:7; James 2:23).

The role of the teacher in this might be called a parental role. The role is easy enough to see in grammar school and even secondary school where the teacher may spend more time maintaining discipline than teaching. In higher education, it is more common to call the teacher a mentor, especially at the graduate level. Here the teacher teaches the student whatever s/he can and then the mentor, at least the good ones, facilitates the student's growth to higher things. If the student merely equals the teacher in knowledge, the teacher has not done a good job. The student's responsibility is to grow beyond the teacher. A good student in turn, will appreciate the facilitator role and live with the awareness that in some sense s/he stands on the mentor's shoulders. The poor student, of course, will get sophomoritis...

A parable caught this concern rather neatly.

Once upon a time, there was a man and he was the strongest man on earth. He had a little son whom he loved very much, and every day they would go out to wrestle. Every day the father would manage to turn the little boy upside down, and at night he would return home carrying the little boy on his shoulders. They both got very sweaty and dirty and had a lot of fun. As the little boy grew older, his skill increased, which was they way it was supposed to be. When he was about 18 years of age, he and his father went out to wrestle in the spirit of comradeship which they had long ago established. They wrestled long and hard. With a particular twist which he had been practicing, the young man threw his father. To his amazement, the older man fell on his back. The young man stood

116

there alone, tears pouring down his cheeks. He had just overthrown the strongest man on earth. He felt very alone. After what seemed like centuries, the older man leapt to his feet. He put his arm around the shoulders of his son. "Thank you," he said. "You have just given me my crown."[29]

Certainly the sages - Egypt, Mesopotamia and Israel - took seriously their role as surrogate parents. "Listen my son...." (Pr 1:8, 2:1, 3:1, etc.) But keep in mind the opening paragraph of Proverbs which not only speaks of training young people but that the wise may also hear and add to their knowledge and powers of discernment. The modern teacher is called not merely to instruct the young but to develop new knowledge - insight, interpretation, research - that is shared with colleagues. The burgeoning numbers of journals and publications speak to the sharing that is reaching monumental proportions. One the one hand, there seems to be some interest in proving the statement of Qoheleth 12:12 that "of the making of many books there is no end." On the other one may be tempted to some of his pessimism when some suggest the much publishing is lest the scholar perish from his/her job. So publishing today may not be philosophy, "love of wisdom," as much as it is love of financial reward or job security.[30]

Still, at its best, the sharing is an honest sharing with one's colleagues. The students who are daughters and sons today - children of one's mind rather than of the body - are tomorrow's colleagues even as the good biological parent raises children to be colleagues - adults co- functioning in an adult world. Thus the teacher/mentor who is today's parent surrogate is, or should be, tomorrow's colleague.

One could even say we are colleagues today. Jack L. Stotts, president of Austin Presbyterian Theological Seminary, defined colleague as "one who joins with another person in shared work." Student and teacher alike share in their commitment to competency in their field. A Wesley or Methodist tradition is that we are called to solid knowledge and vital piety. To Tertullian's ancient question, "What does Athens have to do with Jerusalem?" we answer, "Everything." The wisdom tradition of Israel and the ancient near east held these two - the intellect and the spirit -

117

together in the common bond of devotion to God or the gods.[31]

Teachers as Grandparents

One could also insist that the teacher/mentor/intellectual parent continues to contribute her or himself. But the contribution goes further through one's students who themselves become sharers in the love of wisdom. And in one degree or another, they become mentors to yet others - the first mentor's intellectual grandchildren. One could argue that the grandson who published Ecclesiasticus or the Wisdom of ben Sirach, was not only the biological descendent but the intellectual heir as well.

We see this intellectual grandfather clause in a number of ways even yet today. Several religious traditions - Buddhism, Sufism, Hasidism, Christian mysticism - are often more concerned with their intellectual lineage than exactitudes of hair splitting dogmas. In a number of academic fields, it is known that so-and-so studied with so-and-so. As an example, the "dean" of American biblical archaeologists was William Foxwell Albright. His intellectual "children" include such notables as G. Ernest Wright, Nelson Glueck, David Noel Freedman, Frank Moore Cross, Jr., Dewey Beegle, Carey A. Moore and many others. They in turn became mentors to another generation of notables such as Paul Lapp, James Sauer, William Dever, Joe Seger and a host of others. These now have intellectual children/colleagues of their own, some of whom already have yet another generation of students/colleagues. It may or may not be of interest that subsequent generations do not always agree with earlier ones. Sometimes new evidence or insight modifies or completely changes earlier views.

One could argue further that such lineage is not limited to those who have actually studied with persons in the chain of mentor/colleague. It can include those who have studied, i.e., read and benefitted from the writings or contact with the persons in direct connection. The preserved materials, both modern and ancient, allows any one of us to share in that love of wisdom.

Concluding Note

That is the closing note for this study. I have not
myself been a direct student of Dr. Sebastian A.
Matczak, like Dr. Joseph McMahon and many others. But
I have been privileged to read some of his many
writings - shared with colleagues all over the world
from his native Poland to the United States to Japan
and many points on the globe. As a modern sage, he
calls to higher wisdom - a global wisdom, a humane
wisdom. But it is a wisdom set in the context of the
divine who created the globe and heaven too, who
created the human and by whose standards,
paradoxically, we determine what is humane.

1. The Hebrew Bible includes the first three. The Greek version known as the Septuagint (LXX) contains the five. The Protestant Bible follows the first and puts the last two books in the Apocrypha. The Roman Catholic Bible follows the LXX and includes the five in the Old Testament. Thompson, Approaches to the Bible; Syracuse: Center for Instructional Communication, 1967. David Noel Freedman, "Canon of the Old Testament," Interpreter's Dictionary of the Bible [IDB], Supplementary Volume [SV]; Nashville: Abingdon, 1976, pp. 130-136.

2. James L. Crenshaw, Old Testament Wisdom; Atlanta: Knox, 1981, pp. 245, 37. Idem., "Wisdom in the OT," IDBSV-952-956. Idem., "The Wisdom Literature," pp. 369-407 in The Hebrew Bible and Its Modern Interpreters ed. Douglas A. Knight and Gene M. Tucker; Philadelphia and Chico, CA: Fortress and Scholars Press, 1985. Georg Fohrer, "Sophia," Kittel's Theological Dictionary of the New Testament; Grand Rapids: Eerdmans, 1971, VII:476-496. Robert C. Denton, "Heart," IDB 2 (1962), 549-550. H.-P. Muller, "chakham," in Theological Dictionary of the Old Testament ed G. Johannes Botterweck and Helmer Ringgren; Grand Rapids, MI: Eerdmans, 1980, IV:370-385.

3. Roland E. Murphy, "A Consideration of the Classification 'Wisdom Psalms'," Vetus Testamentum Supplement 9 (1962), 156-167. He notes considerable debate as to which psalms are wisdom psalms or if there even is such a classification. The Listening Heart ed. Kenneth G. Hoglund, et al.; Sheffield: JSOT, 1987. Donn F. Morgan, Wisdom in the Old Testament Traditions; Atlanta: Knox, 1981, pp. 120-136. Sandra Beth Berg, The Book of Esther; Missoula, MT: Scholars, 1977. Robert Gordis, "Religion, Wisdom and History in the Book of Esther - A New Solution to an Ancient Crux," JBL 100 (S 81), 359-388. Carey A. Moore, Esther; Garden City: Doubleday, 1971, p. LII. Shemaryahu Talmon, "Wisdom in the Book of Esther," Vetus Testamentum 13 (1963), 419-455. On Daniel, see "The Tale of Aqhat," pp. 149-155 in James B. Pritchard, Ancient Near Eastern Texts Related to the Old Testament, 3rd ed; Princeton: Princeton University, 1969, pp. 405-440, 589-604. Cited

hereafter as ANET. Muller, op. cit., pp. 376-378.
Sheldon H. Blank, "Wisdom," IDB 4:853-861. Louis F.
Hartman and Alexander A. De Lella, The Book of
Daniel; Garden City: Doubleday, 1978. For the view
that these and the following are not wisdom materials,
see James L. Crenshaw, ed., Studies in Ancient
Israelite Wisdom; NY: KTAV, 1976, pp. 9-13. Gerald H.
Wilson also questions the identification of Daniel with
wisdom material. "Wisdom in Daniel and the Origin of
Apocalyptic," Hebrew Annual Review 9 (1985), 373-381.

4. Blank, op. cit., p. 854. Morgan, op. cit., pp.
30-52. Muller, op. cit., pp. 373-378. Gerhard von
Rad, "The Joseph Narrative and Ancient Wisdom," pp.
292-300 in The Problem of the Hexateuch and Other
Essays; NY: McGraw-Hill, 1966. George W. Coats, "The
Joseph Story and Ancient Wisdom: A Reappraisal," CBQ
35 (1973), 285-297. Muller, op. cit. Crenshaw, OT
Wisdom, op. cit., pp. 40-41 with bibliography. Luis
Alonso-Schokel, "Sapiential and Covenant Themes in
Genesis 2-3," pp. 468-480 in Crenshaw, Studies.., op.
cit. Carole Fontaine, "The Bearing of Wisdom on the
Shape of 2 Samuel 11-12 and 1 Kings 3," Journal for
the Study of the Old Testament No. 34 (F 86), 61-77.
Leonidas Kalugila, The Wise King: Studies in Royal
Wisdom as Divine Revelation in the Old Testament and
Its Environment; Lund: Gleerup, 1980, pp. 104-106.
Walter A. Brueggeman, In Man We Trust; Richmond: Knox,
1972. For JEPD, the idea that the Pentateuch is edited
from four documents, see the classical formulation of
the hypothesis by Julius Wellhausen, Prolegomena to the
History of Ancient Israel; Cleveland: World, 1965
(original 1878).

5. Blank, op. cit., pp. 853-4. Morgan, op. cit., pp.
63-119. William McKane, Prophets and Wise Men;
Naperville, IL: Allenson, 1965. Johannes Fichtner,
"Isaiah Among the Wise," pp. 429-438 in Crenshaw,
Studies.., op. cit. John L. McKenzie, Second Isaiah;
Garden City: Doubleday, 1968, pp. 18, 92, 171. Dennis
J. McCarthy, "Be Sober and Watch," pp. 354-362 in
Intuition and Narrative: Collected Essays
[McCarthy's]; Rome: Biblical Institute, 1985 [Isaiah's
use of wisdom material]. J. William Whedbee, Isaiah and
Wisdom; Nashville: Abingdon, 1971. Samuel Terrien,
"Amos and Wisdom," pp. 108-115 in Israel's Prophetic
Heritage ed Bernhard W. Anderson and Walter
Harrelson, 1962. Hans W. Wolff, Amos the Prophet;
Philadelphia: Fortress, 1973. George M. Landes,

"Jonah: A 'Mashal'?," pp. 137-158 in Israelite Wisdom: Theological and Literary Essays in Honor of Samuel Terrien ed John Gammie, et al.; Missoula, MT: Scholars, 1978.

6. Crenshaw, OT Wisdom, op. cit., pp. 42-54. Robert B.Y. Scott, "Solomon and the Beginnings of Wisdom in Israel," Vetus Testamentum Supplement 3 (1955), 262-279. Albrecht Alt, "Solomonic Wisdom," pp. 102-112 in Crenshaw, Studies.., op. cit. E.W. Heaton, Solomon's New Men; NY: Pica, 1974. Kalugila, op. cit., pp. 106-122.

7. A.F. Butsch, ed., Strassburger Rathselbuch (The Strassburg Book of Riddles); Strassburg: Trubner, 1876. Quoted by Crenshaw, OT Wisdom, op. cit., pp. 43-44. Lou H. Silberman, "The Queen of Sheba in Judaic Tradition," pp. 65-81 in Solomon and Sheba ed. James B. Pritchard; London: Phaidon, 1974, describes a number of these legends.

8. Bernhard W. Anderson, Understanding the Old Testament, 4th ed.; Englewood Cliffs, NJ: Prentice-Hall, 1986, pp. 568-603. John Bright, A History of Israel, 3rd ed.; Philadelphia: Westminster, 1981, p. 220. Modern scholarship is well represented in the Anchor Bible commentaries (Garden City, NY: Doubleday). R.B.Y. Scott, Proverbs - Ecclesiastes, 1965. Marvin H. Pope, Job, 3rd ed; 1973. David Winston, The Wisdom of Solomon; 1979. M. Hadas, "Wisdom of Solomon," IDB 4 (1962), 861-863.

9. The academy founded by Johanan ben Zakkai after he escaped from the destruction of Jerusalem in 70 A.D., was probably more of a discussion center than a voting legislature. The closing of the Hebrew canon probably spread over some time. It is of interest, however, that while considerable amounts of non-canonical materials were found among the Dead Sea Scrolls at Qumran, destroyed c. 68 A.D., none were found among the materials in the Wadi Muraba'at from the time of Bar Koseba, c. 132-135 A.D. On canon, see Jack P. Lewis, "What Do We Mean by Jabneh?" Journal of Bible and Religion XXXII (1964), 125-132. Samuel Sandmel, The Hebrew Scriptures; NY: Knopf, 1963, p. 14, n. 6. Frank M. Cross, The Ancient Library of Qumran and Modern Biblical Study; Garden City, NY: Doubleday, 1961. James A. Sanders, Torah and Canon; Philadelphia: Fortress, 1972. idem., Canon and Community: A Guide to Canonical

Criticism; Philadelphia: Fortress, 1984. Gerald T. Sheppard, "Canonization: Hearing the Voice of the same God through Historically Dissimilar Traditions," Interpretation 36 (Ja 82), 21-33.

10. Thompson, Approaches, op. cit. Eduard Nielsen, Oral Tradition; Naperville, IL: Allenson, 1954. Robert C. Culley, ed., "Oral Tradition and Old Testament Studies," Semeia 5 (1976), 1-163.

11. M. Kraus, "chakham. I. Ancient Near East," pp. 364-370 in Botterweck and Ringgren, op. cit. Martin Noth and D. Winton Thomas, eds., Wisdom in Israel and in the Ancient Near East; Leiden: Brill, 1960. ANET-405-440. Crenshaw, OT Wisdom, op. cit, pp. 212-235. Fohrer, op. cit., pp. 477-480. Kalugila, op. cit., 12-68. Glendon E. Bryce, A Legacy of Wisdom: The Egyptian Contribution to the Wisdom of Israel; Lewisburg, PA: Bucknell, 1979. Adolf Erman, The Ancient Egyptians; NY: Harper & Row, 1966. W.G. Lambert, Babylonian Wisdom Literature; Oxford: Clarendon, 1969. William K. Simpson, ed., The Literature of Ancient Egypt; New Haven: Yale, 1973. Kenneth Cragg, comp., The Wisdom of the Sufis; NY: New Directions, 1976. Jeffrey Hopkins, ed., The Wisdom of Tibet; London: Allen & Unwin, 1977. Yutang Lin, The Wisdom of China and India; NY: Modern Library, 1955. Irmgard Schloegl, tr., The Wisdom of Zen; NY: New Directions, 1976. See the Journal of the American Oriental Society 101, No. 1 (1981) for essays in these several areas.

One can add that wisdom did not end with the Tenak but continued in the Talmud - the Mishnah (c. 200 A.D.) and Gemara (Jerusalem, c. 400 A.D.; Babylonian, c. 500 A.D. Ephraim E. Urbach, The Sages: Their Concepts and Beliefs, 2 vols.; Jerusalem: Magnes Press, Hebrew University, 1975 (original 1969). Jacob Neusner, Our Sages, God, and Israel; Chappaqua, NY: Rossel Books, 1984. The main text here is the Jerusalem or Palestinian Talmud. Neusner notes, p. vii, that the sages joined stout heart to rigorous mind. They demonstrate emotion tamed by criticism, the will shaped by mind, that we are sentient yet thinking beings. Pirke Aboth, the Sayings of the Fathers, is a major example of the continuing wisdom tradition. The sayings of Jesus formed one of the sources of the Christian gospels, called Quelle from the German word for source. The Gospel of Thomas, found with the Nag

Hammadi materials, is a collection of Jesus' teachings. Joseph Blenkinsopp, Wisdom and Law in the Old Testament; NY: Oxford, 1983, pp. 155-156.

12. Thompson, Biblical Archaeology; NY: Paragon House, 1987, pp. 43-46.

13. Anderson, op. cit., p. 589. R.J. Williams, "Wisdom in the Ancient Near East," IDBSV-949-952. Carole R. Fontaine, "A Modern Look at Ancient Wisdom: The Instruction of Ptahhotep Revisited," Biblical Archaeologist 44, No. 3 (Sum 81), 155-160.

14. Harrelson, "Wisdom and Pastoral Theology, ANQ 7 (1966), 6-14. Crenshaw, OT Wisdom, op. cit., pp. 190-191, 210-211.

15. Anderson, op. cit., p. 568. Fohrer, op. cit., p. 478.

16. Abraham H. Maslow, Toward a Psychology of Being; Princeton, NJ: Van Nostrand, 1962. Viktor E. Frankl, Man's Search for Meaning; NY: Beacon, 1963. Eric Berne, Transactional Analysis in Psychotherapy; NY: Grove, 1961. Idem., Games People Play; NY: Grove, 1964.

17. The Fellowship for Spiritual Understanding, P.O. Box 816, Palos Verdes Estates, CA 90274.

18. The ending of Qoheleth is often seen as a later addition by some orthodox editor trying to offset the pessimism of the rest of the book. This may very well be. However, such pessimism is not unknown in wisdom literature, past or present. And in the end, more than one pessimist has thrown up his hands and left it to God or "life's little inequities." Scott, op. cit., p. 256.

19. Walther Eichrodt, Theology of the Old Testament; Philadelphia: Westminster, 1967, Vol. II:81. G. Ernest Wright, God Who Acts; Naperville: Allenson, 1952, p. 103. Gerhard von Rad, Wisdom in Israel; Nashville: Abingdon, 1972, pp. 61-62, claims that Israel had one world of experience with the secular mixed with the sacred. However, in Old Testament Theology; NY: Harper & Row, 1962, 355-359, he could not fit the wisdom material anywhere except with the psalms as Israel's response to God. Frederick M. Wilson rightly protests

creating a biblical theology that focuses on one part of the Bible and then says another part does not fit. "Sacred and Profane? The Yahwistic Redaction of Proverbs Reconsidered," pp. 314-334 in Hoglund, op. cit. Alan W. Jenks, "Theological Presuppositions of Israel's Wisdom Literature," Horizons in Biblical Theology 7, No. 1 (1985), 43-75. For a thorough review of the problems see John Priest, "Wisdom and Humanism, pp. 263-279 in The Answers Lie Below: Essays in Honor of Lawrence Edmonds Toombs ed Henry O. Thompson; Washington: University Press of America, 1984.

20. Fohrer, op. cit., pp. 478-479. Andrew Greeley and Michael Hout have suggested secular society is a myth. They base their claim on the consistency of church attendance over the past 50 years in the U.S. "The Center Doesn't Hold: Church Attendance in the United States, 1940-1984," American Sociological Review 50, No. 3 (June 87), 325-345. Others would claim that there is more to the secular society than church attendance. Gabriel Vahanian, God is Dead; NY: Braziller, 1960.

21. Claudia V. Camp, "Woman Wisdom as Root Metaphor: A Theological Consideration," pp. 45-76 in Hoglund, op. cit. Idem., Wisdom and the Feminine in the Book of Proverbs; Sheffield: Almond, 1985. Carole R. Fontaine, "Queenly Proverb Performance: The Prayer of Puduhepa," pp. 95-126 in Hoglund, op. cit. James G. Williams, Woman Recounted; Sheffield: Almond, 1982.

22. Claudia V. Camp, "The Wise Women of 2 Samuel: A Role Model for Women in Early Israel," CBQ 43 (1981), 14-29. ANET-420-421.

23. ANET-159-223. Fohrer, op. cit., pp. 493-494. Lawrence E. Toombs, "Old Testament Theology and the Wisdom Literature," Journal of Bible and Religion 23, No. 3 (July 55), 193-196. J. Coert Rylaarsdam, Revelation in Jewish Wisdom Literature; Chicago: University of Chicago, 1946, p. 1. Blenkinsop, op. cit., pp. 83 et passim. He cites even earlier laws such as Ur-nammu's before 2000 B.C., and the concern these laws had for justice and protecting the disadvantaged such as the orphan and the widow and the poor.

24. It was discovered by the French Expedition in 1901.

For pictures see James B. Pritchard, The Ancient Near East in Pictures Relating to the Old Testament; Princeton: Princeton University, 1954, Numbers 244, 246, 515. For a translation, ANET-163-180.

26. Scott, op. cit., p. 33, has a dash or pause and begins vs 2 with "for..." Blenkinsop, op. cit., p. 11.

27. Rylaarsdam, op. cit., p. 90. See Romans 2:14 in the Bible. Anthony Battaglia, Toward a Reformulation of Natural Law; NY: Seabury, 1981. Eric D'Arcy, "Natural Law," pp. 1131-1137 in Encyclopedia of Bioethics ed. Warren T. Reich; NY: Free Press, 1978. John Kemp, Ethical Naturalism; NY: St. Martin's, 1970. Lawrence Kohlberg, Essays on Moral Development. Vol. 1 (1981): The Philosophy of Moral Development, and, Vol. 2 (1984): The Psychology of Moral Development; San Francisco: Harper & Row. William A. Spurrier, Natural Law and the Ethics of Love; Philadelphia: Westminster, 1974.

28. Pope, op. cit., pp. 3-6, notes Edom or the Hauran south of Damascus, east of the Sea of Galilee. Scott, op. cit., 175-184, 135-149. Crenshaw, OT Wisdom, op. cit., p. 36, 220. ANET-421-424.

29. Joyce E. Thompson and Henry O. Thompson, Ethics in Nursing; NY: Macmillan, 1981. Idem., Bioethical Decision Making for Nurses; Norwalk, CT: Appleton-Century-Crofts, 1985.

30. Quoted by Pat Crossman, Transactional Analysis Journal 7, No. 1 (Jan 77), 106.

31. Blank, op. cit., p. 856.

32. Stotts, "In Gratitude," Austin Presbyterian Theological Seminary, Annual Report (Spr 86), 1.

ADDITIONAL BIBLIOGRAPHY

Dianne Bergant, What Are They Saying About Wisdom Literature?; NY: Paulist, 1984.

J.A. Emerton, "Wisdom," pp. 214-237 in Tradition and Interpretation ed G.W. Anderson; Oxford: Clarendon, 1979.

Roland E. Murphy, Introduction to the Wisdom Literature of the Old Testament; Collegeville, MN: Liturgical Press, 1965.

___, Wisdom Literature; Grand Rapids: Eerdmans, 1981.

John Paterson, The Book that is Alive; NY: Scribner's, 1964.

___, The Wisdom of Israel; Nashville: Abingdon, 1961.

Orvid S. Rankin, Israel's Wisdom Literature; NY: Schocken, 1969 (original 1936).

Harry Ranston, The Old Testament Wisdom Books and Their Teaching; London: Epworth, 1930.

Robert B.Y. Scott, The Way of Wisdom in the Old Testament; NY: Macmillan, 1971.

Roger N. Whybray, The Intellectual Tradition in the Old Testament; NY: De Gruyter, 1974.

James Wood, Wisdom Literature; London: Duckworth, 1967.

CYRIL LOUKARIS: A PROTESTANT PATRIARCH

OR A PIONEER ORTHODOX ECUMENIST?

Constantine N. Tsirpanlis

Prolegomena

The year 1988 marks the 350th anniversary of Patriarch Loukaris' tragic death (June 27, 1638). It was a most unfortunate and undeserving termination of a "neo-martyr" church leader's life. His life was permeated by ecclesiastico-political problems, intrigues, adversities and controversies, but also by significant cultural, educational and liturgical reforms.[1]

It is appropriate if not imperative to offer this study as a humble homage to the memory of "one of the greatest ecclesiastico-political figures in the 17th century Orthodox East."[2] It is a re-assessment of Loukaris' position in, and contribution to, East - West church and cultural rapproachment, to contemporary ecumenism in general, and to the recent Orthodox-Reformed dialogue in particular.

Biographical Sketch

Cyril Loukaris was born in 1572 in Heraklion, Crete. His uncle was Meletios Pigas (1549-1601),[3] the reputable Patriarch of Alexandria and the most competent theologian of his time. With the assistance of his uncle, the gifted, but very young (12 years old), Cyril traveled first to Italy (Venice, 1584 and Padua, 1589-1592) where he studied theology and philosophy in Greek, Latin, and Italian under the outstanding Greek scholar Maximos Margounios.[4] After Cyril had returned from Italy to Alexandria (1592), he was sent again by his uncle, Patriarch Meletios, who was locus tenens also of Constantinople in 1595,[5] to Poland (1594-95) as Exarch of the Patriarchate of Alexandria with the very difficult task of preventing the Union of the Ukranian Orthodox with Rome (Brest-Litowsk, 1595-1596).

The king of Poland, Sigismund III (1587-1632), had already tried his utmost to impose the Roman Catholic faith upon both the Protestants and the Orthodox of his territory.[6] The lamentable illiteracy, incompetence in leadership and immorality of the Orthodox clergy in Poland helped Sigismund's efforts to Romanize the country.[7] The famous Patriarch of Constantinople, Jeremias II Tranos,[8] had paid a special visit to Poland in 1588 on his way to Moscow. But he could not really help the situation there, even with his gifted ecclesiastical flexibility and diplomacy. Loukaris worked hard for five years in Poland (1594-1599), traveling throughout its cities and villages.[9] It was in Poland that Cyril had his first unpleasant experience and actual fights with Roman Catholic clergy and civil authorities. Loukaris was there in 1595 and 1596 when the Ukranian bishops consummated the Union with Rome in Brest-Litowsk and the "Uniate Orthodox Church of Poland" was founded.

Because of Cyril's bitter opposition to Roman prosylitism in Poland, the Jesuits had already (1595) accused him of being a Calvinist or a Lutheran. According to Pigas' correspondence,[10] such rumors and slanders, spread by the Jesuits, were quite common in Alexandria, Constantinople and even in Crete by 1600. Cyril was the target of some assassination attempts in Poland, Constantinople and Crete.[11]

In spite of these adversities, Loukaris contributed decisively to the solid establishment of the Orthodox Brothers in Russia, Ukraine, Lithuania and Poland, and to the growth and efficient operation of Greek Orthodox schools, especially in Poland.[12] Loukaris worked in Wilna (1595) for 20 months as director of its Greek Orthodox school. He also established the first Greek printing shop there.[13] It published several anti-Latin treatises, some letters addressed to the Russian brotherhoods and one book against the Jews (in Greek and Slavonic, 1593) written by Meletios Pigas.[14]

Loukaris had founded and organized in Lwow the first Greek schools (January or February, 1596).[15] During his five years' service in Poland and the Ukraine, he was frequently forced to interrupt his work and go back to Alexandria, Constantinople and Greece (Thrace and Crete) because of bitter opposition, assassination threats and his poor health.[16] The contemporary Calvinist theologian Antoine Leger reported that Cyril's colleague, Nicephoros Cantacuzenos, the Exarch of the Patriarch of Constantinople in Poland, was killed by Sigismund's order.[17] Leger also reports that Cyril would have been killed if he had not taken refuge in the fortress of Prince Constantine Basil Ostrogsky of Ostrog. Loukaris spent considerable time there until early 1601.[18]

Meletios Pigas had already written to Loukaris in 1594, that "The Orthodox Church in Poland is in greater distress because of the Papal attacks on it. So stay in that country. Do not desert it. And above all, do not be simply an observer of their wicked attempts to destroy our religion. You must take part in the struggle, and show yourself to be a strong and keen contestant, a man of wisdom, a man to be reckoned with."[16]

Loukaris himself gives interesting information in his letter to a certain Cyprian, the archdeacon of Ostrog.[20] During those troubled years in Poland he read Thomas Aquinas and the Greek historian Kedrinos.[21]

In late 1599, Loukaris' aged and suffering uncle Meletios wrote to him asking for his quick return to Alexandria.[22] However, before Cyril left Poland (January 1601), he had to face another attack from the Jesuit abbot of Poland, Peter Scarga. Scarga fabricated a letter from Cyril, addressed to the Roman Catholic bishop of Lwow, Dimitri Solikowski. In that letter Cyril was presented as saying that reunion between the Eastern and Roman Churches was not difficult and could be realized soon and that he accepted the primacy of the pope and the corruption of the Reformers.[23] Of course he protested vehemently against such a forgery.[24]

In his travels, he stopped in Translyvania for theological discussions with the Protestant theologian, Marco Fuchs.[25] From a letter of Loukaris[26] we learn that he addressed to Fuchs two treatises in which Cyril defended the invocation and veneration of saints. These treatises may have originated in the Transylvania encounter. However, that encounter was not Loukaris' first such experience. He had already come into contact with Reformed teachers in Italy and Poland as his correspondence with David Heoschel and Friedrich

131

Sylburg indicates.[27]

From Transylvania, Cyril visited the Greek Orthodox communities in Romania where he delivered several sermons.[28] Finally, he arrived in Egypt on September 11, 1601. Two days later, his uncle Meletios Pigas died.[29] In 1601 or in early 1602, Loukaris was unanimously elected Patriarch of Alexandria. After almost 20 years in that post (except for one year, 1612, in Constantinople),[30] he was chosen to be the ecumenical Patriarch of Constantinople (1620-1638).

Again, the aim of the present paper, as stated in the "Prolegomena," is not to give a complete biography of Loukaris, but a re-evaluation of his contribution to East - West rapproachment and to contemporary ecumenism. However, that cannot be rightly done without first understanding the politico-ecclesiastical circumstances and conflicts in Constantinople at the beginning of the seventeenth century.

The Politico-Ecclesiastical Background of

Seventeenth Century Constantinopole

On 4 Nov 1620,[31] Loukaris was regularly elected Patriarch of Constantinople. By that year, the Church of Constantinople was immersed in bitter controversies, jealousies, illiteracy, superstitions, immorality, poverty, and political conflicts. This was mainly because of the commercial, political and religious interests of the Western powers, France, Venice, England, Austria and Holland. They each sought to have the most influence on the Ottoman administration by using the Patriarch of Constantinople. They strengthened the resistance of the Eastern Church either against Rome (England and Holland) or against the Protestants (France, Venice, Austria and of course the Jesuits). Note that the Patriarch of Constantinople could be removed from office at any time by the Sultan who was de facto the decisive authority in Patriarchal elections.

In such a climate, Cyril could not but be often challenged, persecuted, falsely accused and exiled. He was deposed and restored five times between 1623-1638. Finally his opponents, especially his malicious and envious colleague, Cyril Kontaris, and the Papal

Congregatio de propaganda fide,[32] convinced the Ottoman authorities that he was a conspirator and traitor. They executed him and threw his corpse in the Bosphorus on 27 June, 1638.[33]

Cyril was profoundly convinced that a union with Rome would destroy the institutional and ethnic identity and independence of the Orthodox Church.[34] He had already personally experienced the painful Union of Brest (1596) where the Unia was born as a warning and threat against the independence of Orthodoxy.[35] He became more embittered against the intentions of Rome. He did not hesitate to employ political strategies. In these, he hoped to involve not only the Ottoman Empire itself, but also England, Holland, Sweden and even Venice. He corresponded with the English ambassador Thomas Rowe,[36] the Dutch envoy Cornelius Haga, the king of Sweden Gustav Adolfus,[37] and the king of England Carolus I.[38] These letters provide substantial evidence of Cyril's struggle to limit the effect of the Counter-Reformation, and to stop the expansion of the Catholic West into Orthodox territory.

Now, whether those strategies and the philo-calvinist attitude and theological statements of Loukaris were a rooted in a deeper conviction or not, it is very difficult to say. However, he seems convinced and determined throughout his published correspondence and sermons[39] that his task was to work for the reform of the Orthodox Church. This was not in respect to its dogmas and faith, but to its educational, liturgical and administrative system and to spiritual life, primarily of the clergy. Thus, in 1627 a printing press from England arrived in Constantinople. The Patriarchal Academy in Constantinople was reorganized (1625). A cathechism and a translation of the New Testament in modern Greek were planned.[40] In the end, only the translation appeared, in 1638 after the death of Cyril. Several tractates were printed before his death to counter Roman "propaganda." The result, however, was that the French envoy convinced the Sultan to confiscate the press.

Loukaris' reform program originated in the early years of his Alexandria patriarchate. Already in 1610 we find in Cyril's sermons citations form Calvin's Institutes.[41] In Alexandria (1602), Cyril met Cornelius Haga from whom he received the first theological publications of the Reformed Churches.[42]

And in 1613 Cyril began his correspondence with the
notable Dutch theologian J. Uyttenbogaert who succeeded
Jacob Arminius as head of the famous Arminian
theological school.[43]

In 1618 Cyril stated in a letter[44] that after a
three year struggle, he had "recognized the Reformers'
cause as more righteous and more agreeable with the
teaching of Christ." This letter (besides the many
letters of Loukaris to David le Leuden Wilhem, 1617-
1619) was addressed to a convert from Catholicism to
Protestantism. This was the former Archbishop Marco
Antonio de Dominis. The letter is perhaps the best
illustration and evidence of how extensively the mind
of Loukaris was influenced (by 1618) by Reformation
literature and theological ideas.

He almost rejects church tradition, the Orthodox
view of baptism, of good works as absolutely necessary
for salvation, and the invocation or veneration of the
Saints. However, he continued to believe that icons
rightly used are helpful in prayer. He has in mind, of
course, the thick contemporary ignorance, superstition,
and abuses of icons by ordinary people as well as by
the uneducated clergy. He had frequently complained of
the latter's low standards, illiteracy and immorality.

In 1617,[45] Loukaris sent his son-in-God,
Metrophanes Kritopoulos, to study at Oxford. After
seven years (1617-1624), Loukaris asked Kritopoulos to
travel through Germany and Switzerland, to familiarize
himself with the Reformed Churches of Europe, before
returning to Constantinople. Kritopoulos visited
Basel, Bern, Geneva, Zurich, Schaffhausen, St. Gallen,
and Chur in 1627. While Kritopoulos felt the necessity
of a rapprochement with the Reformed Churches, he did
not share Reformation ideas as fully as Cyril. That
may have been the main reason Kritopoulos condemned his
master and spiritual father Loukaris, for
"Protestantism," in a local synod in Constantinople in
1638, after Cyril's death. At that time, Metrophanes
was already Patriarch of Alexandria. Metrophanes had
already written (1625) his Confessio Fidei, which is
the most concise and comprehensive statement of Eastern
Orthodox Faith after the fall of Constantinople
(1453).[46]

Loukaris as Church Reformer: The "Confession"

134

Lukas Vischer, with whom I essentially agree, writes that in Loukaris' "understanding Reformed doctrine was suited to bring the 'true' Orthodoxy to light."[47]

In 1628, Antoine Leger arrived at Constantinople (from Geneva) to assume the vital post of Chaplain to the Dutch Embassy on the request of Cornelius Haga. Leger became very active and influential in promoting Loukaris' rapprochement to the Reformers and supporting him in his policies. But he also organized and spread Protestant missions and schools in the territories of the Patriarchates of Jerusalem and Alexandria. Leger's role was decisive in shaping the final text of Loukaris' "confession" and in making it known to both the churches of the Orthodox East and the Latin West.[48]

Loukaris said in an unpublished letter to Leger (1628)[49] that he had received two copies of the "confession," which Leger had composed and sent to be approved and signed by the Patriarch. Indeed, after Cyril had approved and signed them, he sent them to Haga who forwarded both copies to France.

In March, 1628, with the support of the English ambassador Thomas Rowe,[50] Loukaris succeeded in convincing the Ottoman administration to expel, at least temporarily, the Jesuits form Constantinople. The Dutch ambassador Haga was also quite influential in eliminating papal persecution of the Orthodox Church, according to Loukaris's own testimony.[51] Thus the evidence is more than clear on the motivation of Loukaris' political and religious alliance with the Reformed powers in Constantinople and in Europe. In other words, the alliance was aimed at stopping Roman Catholic propaganda and expansion in the East rather than at a "doctrinal renewal or reform" of the Orthodox Church.

Unfortunately, Loukaris' deeper motivation was not properly understood nor appreciated, neither by his contemporaries nor by today's theologians and churchmen.

Loukaris' "Confession" was condemned as non-Orthodox or as Calvinist "heresy." Loukaris was accused of being a Calvinist "heretic" (1638 synod) by six local synods in the East: Constantinople (1638, 1642, 1672, 1691), Jassy (1642), and Jerusalem (1672). In addition, two special "Confessions of Orthodox Faith" were written by Peger Mogila (the Metropolitan of Kiev, 1638-1642) and by the Patriarch of Jerusalem, Dositheos (1672), in order to refute the "Confession" of Loukaris. These two are generally accepted by all Eastern Orthodox Churches as so-to-speak <u>Regulae Fidei</u>. But it is extremely important to also point out a special aspect. According to the council of Jerusalem (1672), the main reason for the condemnation was Loukaris' refusal to reject in writing the contents of that "Confession" as his own beliefs. He had already taken an oath that he was not the author and that he personally did not believe in those doctrines. On the contrary, he preached the opposite of those contents.[52]

The "Confession" of Cyril was compiled by Leger. It was printed first in Latin, in Geneva, in 1629. The intent was to use it only in the West, not in the East and only for their struggle against Roman Catholics, not for prosylitism. Thus we may conclude that Loukaris fell victim to the Reformers of Geneva, especially of Leger. Under the latter's pressure, the Latin text was translated into Greek and published four years later, in 1633, with the reluctant approval of the Patriarch. Cyril was struggling desperately for survival against his domestic and foreign opponents and so many ecclesiastico-political crises.

Of course, Loukaris was a sympathizer and supporter of the "Reformers' cause" and of certain Calvinist views, i.e. the doctrines of the eucharist, baptism, church tradition, etc. as already mentioned. But he never tried to incorporate or impose his own personal philo-Calvinist views on any public church document, council or official Patriarchal statement of faith. Still it is not clear whether those philo-Calvinist views expressed in Loukaris' letters to so many Reformers, were his own personal convictions or if they were motivated by political and diplomatic objectives.

This question may be answered when Loukaris' numerous letters and sermons are published and available for research. For now, they are still in manuscript form in libraries in Switzerland (Geneva), England, France, Greece (Athens), Constantinople (<u>Methochion tou Panayiou Taphou</u> on the isle of Halke or Heybeliada), The Hague, Moscow, and who knows where else.

Last, but not at least, suppose that the contents of the "Confession" (the 18 chapters plus the 4 questions which he added at the end) were Loukaris' own views. No Orthodox synod or any local Eastern Orthodox church would have ever adopted it. On the contrary, from the beginning, the Church at large (consensus Ecclesiae) and most Orthodox theologians and people (consensus fidelium) have ignored the "Confession" as Protestant doctrine. The exception is chapters 1, 7 and partially the 6th which treat the Orthodox doctrines of the Trinity, the incarnation and original sin.[53]

The "confession" is a Calvinistic text which primarily follows Calvin's basic work Institutio christianae religionis, and secondarily follows the Confessio Gallicana and the Confessio Belgica. Some views in several chapters of the "Confession" are closer to Orthodox doctrine. Precisely this fact confirms my opinion that those views were Loukaris' own corrections, changes and amplification of the original text compiled by the Reformed theologians of Geneva. Hence even Loukaris' signature on the Greek text of the "Confession" cannot be used as decisive proof of his so-called "Calvinist conversion." However, he was considerably influenced by the Reformers' ideas on a more efficiently and systematically organized education, liturgical reform (preaching), church administration, and missionary program.

The Contribution of Loukaris to Ecumenism

The contribution of Loukaris to Ecumenism in general, and to the Orthodox-Reformed Dialogue in particular is significant.

Jeremias Tranos[54] of Constantinople was the first to start a theological dialogue with the Lutheran theologians of Tubingen (1573-1581). Cyril Loukaris was the first Orthodox Patriarch to develop a practical and heartistic relationship and collaboration with the theological and political leadership of the Reformed Church. Loukaris and Kritopoulos, whose masterpiece Confession of Orthodox Faith[55] helped many Protestants understand and appreciate Eastern Orthodoxy, can be called pioneer Orthodox ecumenists and the chief forerunners among the Orthodox of our contemporary Ecumenical Movement.

True, the decisive and more complete response of Orthodoxy to the great challenge of Calvinism and of the Reformation in general, was the Confession of Dositheos,[56] the Patriarch of Jerusalem. To this we can add the decisions and decrees of the Orthodox Synod in Jerusalem (1672) in which Dositheos presided. However, without the work, activity and encouragement of Loukaris, Dositheos, nor for that matter, Kritopoulos, would not have been challenged. Perhaps they would not have been inspired to write their own Confession. Dositheos' Confession is a point-for-point rejection of Loukaris' "Confession." Five chapters in the Confession of Dositheos are devoted to showing that Loukaris could not have written a Calvinistic confession. Numerous citations from Cyril's writings and sermons are used by Dositheos to demonstrate that Cyril's "Confession" does not correspond to Cyril's own beliefs.

Another fundamental contribution of Loukaris to the Ecumenical Movement and particularly to the Orthodox - Reformed Dialogue is the occasional clarification and appreciation (from an Orthodox viewpoint) of certain basic Reformed doctrines. These include the reading and priority of Scripture, the Filioque clause, original sin, the real presence of Christ in the eucharist, the baptismal "remission of sin," the fallibility of the Church and divine predestination and election. The latter in our time has become "less affirmative than was customary,"[57] on the Reformed side than in Loukaris' and Dositheos' times.

Lukas Vischer, again, is not wrong, I think, when he writes recently that, "a reading of the Decrees (he means mainly those of the local Synod of Jerusalem, 1672) shows that certain Reformed formulations were simply misunderstood." "Occasionally the dispute over Kyrill's short and almost too terse formulations led to distortion of the Reformed teaching."[58] But precisely because of those misunderstandings and distortions, not only on the Orthodox side but also on the Reformed side, our contemporary Orthodox - Reformed dialogue must undertake a more serious theological study of the differences, which unfortunately still divide the two Churches.

Loukaris, Dositheos and Kritopoulos are very helpful in providing not only the basic themes of such a study, but also most of the answers. These include such issues as:

1) The Filioque question (the "Confession," articles 1 and 12 (but not Dositheos and Kritopoulos), seems inclined to the Western position of the procession of the Spirit from the Father through the Son).[59]

2) In what sense can there be other intermediaries (Mary, the saints) besides the "sole mediator (Christ) between God and man" (article 8)? In other words, is the Church the source of Divine Grace and salvation or rather its steward and dispenser? (articles 2, 13).

3) Is man saved by faith alone or through faith and works? (Dositheos is most instructive and helpful in these two last extremely difficult questions. Cf. articles 3, 9, 13, 14).

4) What is the value and meaning of free will, synergy and divine grace? (article 14).

5) Is Holy Scripture the sole source of divine revelation? What is the value and meaning of tradition, and the nature and authority of the Church? (articles 2, 10, 11, 12; cf. Loukaris' answers to 1st, 2nd, 3rd and 4th questions).

6) What is the genuine meaning of Reformed doctrine on predestination, Providence and original sin? (articles 3, 4, 5, 6).

7) Are the Sacraments of Baptism and Eucharist (articles 6, 16) and the other Sacraments mere "signs" or "seals" (art. 15, 17) of the divine grace and promise (the Reformed or Cyrilic? view)? Or are they rather tools which necessarily impart grace to those who are initiated in them (Dositheos' and the Orthodox teaching)? How can metousiosis or transubstantiation be interchanged or identified with metabole or metapoiesis, two more traditional Patristic terms, without scholastic connotations and complications? (article 17) And what is the Liturgical and especially the Sacramental function of the priest and bishop (article 10)?

8) Is the Church infallible? (article 2; cf. the answer to the 1st and 3rd question). If it is, in what sense is the Church infallible? An objective re-

evaluation the ecumenicity of the seven Ecumenical Synods is still imperative.

9) What is the meaning of the "middle state" (purgatory) of the soul after death? (article 18).

10) Can an understanding be reached on the legitimacy of icons within church worship? Here both Loukaris and Dositheos say yes.[60]

Conclusion

The greatest lesson we learn from Loukaris' life and work is the great need on both sides, Reformed and Orthodox, of a more serious, objective, scholarly and deeper dialogue. Such a dialogue could be productive if and when both sides reach a deeper understanding the church tradition of the first nine centuries.

The same need is applicable to the Catholic-Orthodox dialogue. If the search for unity is to get anywhere, it will need to heal the old and new wounds of proselytizing among the Orthodox by would-be "missionaries." This healing can be realized through a genuine approach in friendship, with a readiness to forgive and to be forgiven. A consideration of the life and work of Cyril Loukaris leads one to deplore his hostility to Rome and his vision of Christian unity as an "alliance against Rome." But it reminds us that this hostility and its causes are elements in the life of Orthodoxy and Catholicism that need to be healed if a wider unity is to be attained. More positively, Loukaris' pioneering work for unity shows us that at heart it is a common search. We seek through fellowship, through the sharing of insights, through learning from each other's traditions, to deepen and strengthen our common life in Christ.

Certainly, the interfaith or interchurch meetings, discussions and publications, especially the BEM or Lima text of the World Council of Churches have created a friendlier, a more positive and a new climate. This is especially true for ecclesiology. And one must be hopeful, prayerful, and laborious for a more visible, a more genuine and a real church unity. This must be rooted in and based on the Fear of, the Truth of and Love for the Lord: Phobos Kyriou kai Agape en Alethia (John 8:32: 18:37. I John 4:16. I Cor 13: 1-9). This is

Love as the union of truth, glory and kenosis of God or
love crucified (Phil 2:7-9)!

1. The number of books, articles and studies on Loukaris' life and work is enormous. One can note here the most important recent publications. John Karmiris, "The Problem of the So-Called 'Loukarious' Confession," Theologia [Athens, in Greek] 56, No. 4 (1985), 657-693. Idem., 59, No. 2 (1988), 209-229. Colin Davey, "Metrophanes Kritopoulos and Relations Between the Orthodox, Roman Catholic and Reformed Churches," Church and Theology [London] 5 (1984), 303-363, especially 318-319, 351, 357-359. Lukas Vischer, "The Legacy of Kyrill Loukaris: A Contribution to the Orthodox-Reformed Dialogue," Mid-Stream 25, No. 2 (1986), 165-183. Keetje Rosemond, Cyrille Lucar: Sermons (1598-1602); Leiden: Brill, 1974. Rudolph Hotz, Ein calvinistischer Patriarch von Konstaninopel; Zurich: 1984. E. Adamakis, Eight Marilogical Homilies by Kyrillos Loukaris from the codex MPT 424; Brookline, MA: unpublished dissertation, 1987. Id., Cyrille Lucar et la Theologie occidentale; Geneve – Paris: 1988. Gerhard Hering, Oekumenisches Patriarchat aund Uropaische Politik 1620-1638, Wiesbaden: 1968. Steven Runciman, The Great Church in Captivity; Cambridge: Harvard, 1968, especially book III, ch. 6, "The Calvinist Patriarch," pp. 259-288. George A. Hadjiantoniou, Protestant Patriarch: The Life of Cyril Lucaris (1572-1638), Patriarch of Constantinople; London: Epworth, 1961, especially ch. 11, "Confessio Fidei," pp. 91-109; also pp. 141-145 for an English translation. R.J. Roberts, "The Greek Press at Constantinople in 1627 and its Antecedents," The Library [Oxford], Fifth Series 22 (1967), 13-43. G.D. Dragas, "Seventeenth Century Document Relating to the Confessio Fidei..." (e.g., Loukaris), Abba Salama 9 (1978), 153-206, especially pp. 154- 205-206. E. Perret, "Metrophanes Kritopoulos, Kyrillos Loukaris et Geneve (1627-1640)," Church and Theology 2 (1981), 1025-1054.

2. Karmiris seems to evaluate similarly Loukaris' personality, op. cit., 56:667, n. 4 and 59:218, 211.

3. For the background and career of Pigas, see Tsirpanlis, "Church Relations Between Moscow-Constantinople-Alexandria Towards the End of the Sixteenth Century," The Patristic and Byzantine Review 5, No. 3 (1986), 185-195 [hereafter PBR].

4. For Margounios' life and work see Deno J. Geanakoplos, Byzantine East and Latin West; Oxford: 1966, ch. 6.

5. See Methodios Fouyas' publication of Letters of Meletios Pigas [in Greek]; Athens: 1976, pp. 184-185, 181-182, 267-268, 228-230, 278-279, 281 [hereafter LMP].

6. LMP-267.

7. LMP-340, 239-241, 206, 282-283, 274, 270, 202-203, 222-223. See further the letter of Gabriel Dorotheidis addressed to Loukaris on 3 Oct 1596 in E. Legrand, Bibliographie Hellenique du XVII Siecle; Paris: 1894, IV:225-227.

8. Tsirpanlis, "A Prosopography of Jeremias Tranos 1536-1595, and his Place in the History of the Eastern Church," PBR 4, No. 3 (1985), 155-174, especially pp. 163-166.

9. LMP-194-196.

10. LMP-348, 340, 278, 270-272, 200, 184-185.

11. LMP-202-203, 278, 271, 185.

12. LMP-78, 217, 261-263, 278, 339-340, 194-195.

13. LMP-339-340, 202. See also two letters of Dorotheidis in Legrand, op. cit., IV:225-229; and Leger in Th. Smith, Collectanea de Cyrillo Lucario, Patriarcha Constaninopolitano; London: 1707, p. 78.

14. LMP-77, 78, 328-329, 263, 274, 282.

15. LMP-330. This information is provided by a letter of Dorotheidis, 9 Jan 1596, in A.P. Kerameus, Hellenika Keimena, p. 416, and also Pigas' correspondence with the Latin bishop of Lwow, LMP-282-283.

16. LMP-202-203, 199, 184-185, 278, 283, 288-289, 328-330, 333, 339, 340, 348, 194-195, 190-193, 181-182, 66-67. Legrand, op. cit., IV:217, 220, 228-230. See also Leger in Smith, op. cit., pp. 78-79.

17. Smith, op. cit., pp. 78-79.

18. Ibid., p. 79. LMP-289, 286, 328, 92-94, 201, 202, 207, 209, 225.

19. LMP-202.

20. LMP-282-283, 328-329.

21. Legrand, op. cit., IV:220.

22. LMP-272.

23. Rosemond, op. cit., pp. 14-15.

24. Leger in Smith, op. cit., pp. 79-80, 12, 13.

25. The visit to Transylvania may have been on his way back to Alexandria. More likely, it was in 1612. P. Trivier, Cyrille Lucar, sa vie et son influence; Paris: 1877, p. 46. A. Pichler, Geschichte des Protestantismus in der Orientalischen Kirche im 17. Jahrhundert, oder der Patriarch Cyrillus Lucaris und seine Zeit; Munchen: 1862, p. 31. Rosemond, op. cit., pp. 15-16.

26. Dated 6 Sep 1618 in Legrand, op. cit., IV:329-340.

27. Vischer, op. cit., p. 167. C. Davey, 1 (1980), 252.

28. Codex of the Metochion of Constantinople, 408, 58, 73, 81, 84.

29. Leger in Smith, op. cit., p. 80.

30. Davey, op. cit., 1:278 n. 98. Rosemond, op. cit., p. 16.

31. Legrand IV:340-342.

32. Davey, op. cit., 5:318-319 and 1:246-247. Tsirpanlis, "Cyrill Lukaris and the Catholic Propagation of Rome 1622-1638," Kritologia 4 (1977), 49-56.

33. Arnold J. Toynbee, A Study of History; London: 1935-1961, VIII:156. Davey, op. cit., 5:351.

34. This is especially shown in the Pigas - Loukaris correspondence. See Loukaris' letter of 30 Dec 1635 in Georg Hofmann, "Griechische Patriarchen und romische

Papste. Patriarch Kyrillos Loukaris und die Romische Kirche," Orientalia Christiana Periodica 15 (1929), 99 [hereafter OCP].

35. J. Krajcar, "Jesuits and the Genesis of the Union of Brest," OCP 44 (1978), 37-49.

36. Their secret correspondence of 1625-1628 is published by Manoussos Manousakas, Pepraghmena tou 9 Diethn. Byzantin. Syn. Thessalonikes II (1955), 533-544.

37. Chrysostomos Papadopoulos, "Relations of Cyril Loukaris with Gustav Adolfus II of Sweden," Theologia 12 (1934), 289-291 [in Greek].

38. Andreas Tillyrides, "Cyril Lucaris and the Codex Alexandrinus," Analekta [Alexandria] 1 (1975), 103-133.

39. The only available collection of Loukaris' sermons (24 from 1598-1602) is Rosemond, op. cit., with helpful introduction, notes, bibliography and indexes.

40. N. Vaporis, "Patriarch Kyrillos Loukaris and the Translation of the Scriptures into Modern Greek," Ekklesiastikos Pharos 59, Nos. I-IV (1977), 227-241, especially pp. 229, 231, 234, 240.

41. Davey, op. cit., 1:275.

42. Hadjiantonious, op. cit., p. 41.

43. Ibid., pp. 41-43.

44. Legrand IV:329-340.

45. Davey, op. cit., 1:284-285.

46. Karmiris, Ta Dogmatika kai Symbolika Mnemeia tes Orthodoxou Katholikes Ekklesias; Athens: 1953, II:489-561.

47. Vischer, op. cit., p. 168.

48. For the Greek text, cf. Karmiris, Dogmatica II:565-570. The English, as noted, is in Hadjiantoniou, op. cit., pp. 141-145.

49. This letter is in the Geneva Library, gr. 37-38.

Personal communcation, John Karmiris.

50. Manousakas, op. cit., p. 539. Karmiris dates this victory of Loukaris in 1627, in Theologia 56:666, without reference.

51. Hofmann, op. cit., pp. 99-100.

52. Kirmiris, Dogmatika, 2nd ed, II:805-806; 1st ed, II:706-707, 696, 570.

53. Philip Schaff, Creeds of Christendom, 6th ed; NY and London: 1931, I:54, "The Confession of Cyril Lucar was never adopted by any branch or party of the Eastern Church."

54. Tsirpanlis, The Historical and Ecumenical Significance of Jeremias II's Correspondence with the Lutherans, I; NY: American Institute for Patristic and Byzantine Studies, 1982.

55. Greek text, Karmiris, Dogmatika, 1st ed, op. cit., II:498-561.

56. Karmiris, op. cit., pp. 734-773 (text) with the Acts of the synod and introduction, notes and comments, pp. 694-733.

57. Vischer, op. cit., p. 179.

58. Ibid.

59. Karmiris, Ta Dogmatika, op. cit., II:565-566.

60. Ibid., p. 570.

REUNIFICATION AND REBUILDING

Roger W. Wescott

The material with which I hope to support the central
thesis of this presentation comes chiefly from courses
that I have taught in the related fields of comparative
mythology and comparative religion. Immersion in the
literature of these two fields has led me to conclude,
at least tentatively, that myth, even in its
secularized versions, is a fundamental form of
religious discourse and that the unfinished story which
it tells, with endless variations, is one of paradise
suddenly and catastrophically lost, then slowly but
only partially regained. While it is often only
implicit, there is, I find, a basic "mythic mood,"
which, though heavily tinged with both hope and fear,
is overwhelmingly one of nostalgia--the yearning to
recover a half-forgotten harmony of God, Man, and
Nature.

This nostalgia is expressed in much of our
religious terminology. Words like redemption,
resurrection, and reincarnation all express a need to
recapture a condition or repeat a process which is
conceived of as not only prior to the present time but
also preferable to what exists or occurs at present.
All piety revives the past, and all faith involves some
hope or expectation that the past and those who were
part of it (including ourselves) may be "born again."
What such piety and faith further imply is that the
future shares with the past its superiority to the
present, both past and future exhibiting a sacred or
mythic quality that sets them off from the unregenerate
and unholy present.

The very etymology of the religion reinforces this
repetitive theme. Whether we follow majority opinion
in deriving the term from Latin religare, "to tie
back," or minority opinion in deriving it from Latin
relegere, "to gather again," we are faced with a
deverbative noun that emphasizes reaffirmation of

147

ancient truth and return to early values.[1]

In the secular realm, much of which seems to be a denatured derivative of the religious realm, there are also terminological suggestions of a similar nostalgia for vanished life-ways. However far its actual implementation fell short of its goal, the political Reconstruction that followed the American Civil War, for example, had as its ultimate objective the restoration of the civil consensus that had previously held the United States together. Revolution, whether specifically political or generally ideological, has as its most literal meaning the return of time's wheel to its starting point, whereupon a new cycle can be initiated. Recapitulation, finally, even when it refers (controversially) to the tendency of an embryo of one species prenatally to reproduce the adult forms of species ancestral to it, likewise exhibits reference to a former state of things that is somehow revived at a later time.

We see this myth or theme continuing in one of the so-called "new religions." Although the theology of the Unification Church is not as precisely or dogmatically formulated as that of many older religious groups, its main outlines are quite clear. Two of its major tenets are the Principle of Creation and the Principle of Restoration.[2] The first of these involves a belief that God's world was flawlessly formed and that the relation between God and his creatures, including Man, was initially one of complete harmony. The second involves the assumption that Man lost this harmonious relation with God a well as the belief that Man must recover the lost innocence of his prelapsarian state. As stated, these two principles are quite congruent with orthodox Christian doctrine. To the extent that they differ, Unification thought seems more positive in emphasizing the restoration of Edenic bliss where Christianity emphasizes salvation from sin and retribution.

A cursory survey of the world's cosmogonies and anthropogonies[3] further indicates that, with regard to the distinction between restoration and salvation, Unificationism comes slightly closer to the "mythic mainstream" of humanity than does Christianity. Most mythologies describe a primal paradise preceding a catastrophic occurrence that brought humanity low and imply that our collective goal must be reclamation of

148

that paradisal inheritance.

During the past century and a half, the most nearly global trauma to have afflicted the world's indigenous peoples is the process of involuntary Westernization, involving almost complete disruption of their traditional life-ways. To this cultural and psychological shock, many of those peoples reacted with essentially religious responses, creating nativistic cults that anthropologist Anthony Wallace calls "revitalization movements."[4] Two conspicuous examples of such revitalizing efforts are the Ghost Dance of the North American Indians and the cargo cults of Melanesia. In each case, the participating tribal communities were convinced that a great change was imminent--one in which the ancestral order would be restored as suddenly and as cataclysmically as it had previously been subverted by European industrial power.

Such nativistic movements differ little in spirit from religious movements within the Western world of the type known as millenarian or chiliastic, examples being Adventism and Mormonism. While nativists have sought to rid themselves of alien settlers or colonizers, millennialists have sought rather to overcome alien ideologies, such as secularism and materialism, within their own societies.

The cyclical view of time as consisting of a series of creations, destructions, and re-creations is often said to characterize ancient (pre-Christian) societies and modern non-Western societies but to be absent from the modern West, which rather equates the passage of time with the progress of humanity from a lower to a higher state.[5] But, even if we grant that progressivism has been predominant in the Western world since at least the inception of the Industrial Revolution, it seems clear that cyclicism has remained an important, if subordinate, strain in Western thought. An illustration of the persistence of cyclicism is the adoption, in the 19th century, of the term "Medieval" to designate the dark age that was regarded as having put an end to the glory of Greco-Roman civilization yet heralded the equal glory of modern times. Here the perceived pattern was evidently one of creation, destruction, and re-creation or growth, decay and new growth.

This pattern appears or has reappeared in the

149

central text of the Unification Church. Although the
textual interpretation of The Divine Principle appears,
in some sections, to be as problematic as Biblical
exegesis, my inclination is to understand the
tripartite formula "origin-division-union"[6] as
referring to a comparably triune sequence of
integration, dissolution, and re-integration. Here,
despite the fact that unity is not mentioned until the
conclusion of the sequence, I am disposed to think of
it as implied at the outset (by the fact that division
is its apparent negation), so that its terminal
occurrence is actually a recurrence: union is reunion. Such alpha/omega equivalence echoes the Tao Teh
Ching, in which we read that "unity of origin is the
mystery of mysteries, the gateway to spirituality."[7]

My inclination to regard Unification in particular
as part of a larger trend toward reunification in
general is justified, I believe, by the fact that a
majority of the world's mythic traditions treat overt
creation as covert re-creation. More precisely, few
origin-tales portray God or any of various demiurges as
constructing the world from a void.[8] In most creation
narratives, the creative act consists of confronting a
chaotic or dismembered universe (implicitly, that is,
one which has been damaged or partially destroyed) and
reshaping it in such a way as to make it orderly
again--however much the new order may differ from the
old.[9]

The mood of nostalgia which we noted earlier as
being inherent in much religious terminology and some
secular terminology as well goes far beyond formal
language. Even during the most exuberantly optimistic
periods of the expansion of Western civilization, there
has been a persistent under-tone of regret, suggesting
a sense of loss or exile. Aggressively successful
individuals--as represented, for example, by Orson
Welles' Citizen Kane--often retain a secretly wistful
feeling that their childhoods were the best times of
their lives. Aging adults miss "the good old days,"
when life somehow seemed less alienating. And
emigrants who eagerly left their homelands to find
political freedom or economic opportunity in foreign
regions likewise find themselves uprooted and at loose
ends away from "the old country."

If in fact the lives of our preliterate ancestors
were generally as "nasty, brutish, and short" as Thomas

Hobbes and many of his evolutionist successors have supposed, it is difficult to understand why there is such a wide-spread mood of repining and regret among the world's peoples. If, as a species, we have so much to look forward to, why do we spend so much time looking backward? It may be that our persistent backward-looking is in itself evidence of a collective psychic wound in our past and that, as myths themselves assert, our wound was more than psychic. The physical science of our day is taking increasing cognizance of cosmic violence, ranging from black holes through supernovae to the Big Bang which is the astronomers' equivalent of Divine Creation.

True, the scholarship of the past two centuries has generally located such violence outside our solar system. Many solar planets, however, have a battered appearance. The asteroids look like debris from a shattered body. And there is, from the standpoint of uniformitarian science, an embarrassingly abundant amount of evidence for early catastrophes here on earth, ranging from complete animals and trees found in coal-seams[10] to simultaneous destruction of cities from the Mediterranean to the Indian Ocean in the second millennium B.C.[11]

As regards terrestrial disasters, mythology complements science by speaking of global fire, flood, earth-tremors, hurricanes, and falls of boulders from the sky. But it goes beyond science, even of the catastrophist variety, in rhapsodizing about a pre-catastrophic order, which the Biblical tradition called the Garden of Eden and Classical tradition, the Golden Age. If we combine these Mediterranean traditions with others less familiar, we obtain a picture of a primal paradise which differed both physically and behavioral from the world with which we are acquainted. In that world, we are told, there was no winter and no night. People felt lighter than they now do. They were healthier and lived longer. (To make this scenario plausible, we must assume that earth was then a satellite of one of the Jovian planets, on which it had a gravitational and rotational lock such that it never turned one bulging face away from that planet.[12]) Individual egos as we now know them scarcely exist. Instead, humanity took part in a psychic unity that was experiential rather than abstract in nature. Because there was neither material scarcity nor emotional isolation, behavior of the type that we call loving,

151

altruistic, and generous was typical. But it was engaged in naturally and spontaneously rather than, as today, in ambivalent and sporadic response to external moral exhortations and internal guilt feelings.

In Unification doctrine, those elements most reminiscent of this paradisal paradigm are, first, the general emphasis on family unity as opposed to personal self-assertion and, second, the concept of the True Parent, who is to found a God-centered lineage of humanity, as opposed to the flawed parent of history, who perpetuated the self-centered lineage to which most of us still belong. Both the Golden Age tradition and Unification belief here merge with the humanitarian ideal of a Family of Man which, having once been a living reality but having then been fragmented by interethnic conflict, must now be reconstituted.

FOOTNOTES

1. Mircea Eliade, The Myth of the Eternal Return; NY: Pantheon, 1954.

2. M. Darrol Bryant and Susan Hodges, eds., Exploring Unification Theology, Part I, Conversation I: Creation and Fall: NY: Rose of Sharon, 1978. M. Darrol Bryant and Herbert W. Richardson, eds., A Time for Consideration: A Scholarly Appraisal of the Unification Church, Part II, Chapter 1, "A Brief Outline of Unification Theology": NY: Edwin Mellen, 1978.

3. S.G. Youngert, "Cosmogony and Cosmology", in Volume 4 of James Hastings' Encyclopedia of Religion and Ethics: NY: Scribner's, 1908-27. Philip Freund, Myths of Creation: NY: Washington Square Press, 1965, Chapter 10, "man and Totem"

4. Anthony F. Wallace, Religion: An Anthropological View: NY: Random House, 1966.

5. John B. Bury, The Idea of Progress: An Inquiry into its Origin and Growth: London: MacMillan, 1928.

6. The Divine Principle, 5th ed.; NY: The Holy Spirit Association for the Unification of World Christianity, 1977, Part I, Section II, Subsection 3, Infrasection (1) (No author named. The ideas set forth are presumably those of Sun Myung Moon, although the wording is apparently that of anonymous church members and translators.)

7. R.B. Blakney, The Way of Life: A New Translation of the Tao The Ching, NY: New American Library, 1955.

8. Maria Leach, The Beginning: Creation Myths around the World: NY: Funk and Wagnalls, 1956.

9. Alfred L. Kroeber and E.W. Gifford, "World Renewal: A Cult System of Native Northwest California, Anthropological Records 1, No. (1949).

10. William R. Corliss, Unknown Earth: A Handbook of Geological Enigmas, Chapter 4, section 2, subsection 6, "Polystrate Fossils", Glen Arm, MD: The Sourcebook Project, 1980. Derek V. Ager, The Nature of the

Stratigraphical Record, chapter 4, "Catastrophic Stratigraphy"; London: MacMillan, 1973.

11. Claude F. Schaeffer, Stratigraphie Comparee et Chronologies de l'Asie Occidentale: London: Oxford University, 1948.

12. David N. Talbott, The Saturn Myth, Garden City, NY: Doubleday, 1980.

BACK OF THE WRITTEN WORD

Lars Aagaard-Mogensen was trained at Aarhus University
(1963-72) where he received the Filosofikum (1964),
Certificate (1967), Pedagogical Diplomas (1968),
Mag.art. in Philosophy (1972), Lic.theol. in
Philosophical Aesthetics (1980), at SUNY (M.A. in
Philosophy '71), Temple ('72-4 postgraduate studies in
aesthetics). His Lic.theol. dissertation was on
"Epistemic-aesthetic Explorations in Identity and
Difference." He has taught at Aarhus, SUNY, University
of Copenhagen, Hellenic International School, Gent
[Ghent] State University (Belgium),
Washington University (St. Louis), Harvard, St. Cloud
State University (MN), Rochester (NY) Institute of
Technology. He is a member of the American
Philosophical Association, American Society for
Aesthetics, British Society of Aesthetics,
Communication & Cognition, Selskabet for Filosofi og
Psykologi (Copenhagen), American Humor Association,
Scandinavian Society of Aesthetics, etc. He has held
editorial responsibilities with Philosophia
Arhusiensis, Journal of Aesthetics and Art Criticism,
and Restant, and is the recipient of numerous awards
and grants. His bibliography runs to over 100 items and
includes 16 books such as Culture and Art (Nyborg, DK &
Atlantic Highlands, NJ: F. Lokkes Forlag & Humanities
Press, 1976), Om Tolerance (Grenaa, DK: Humanistica
III, 1978), Contemporary Aesthetics in Scandinavia
(with G. Hermeren; Lund: Bokforlaget Doxa, 1980), Our
Art (Gent: Communication & Cognition, 1983), Art in
Culture (with A. Balis, et al.; Gent: C&C, 1985) and
Real Art (Gent: C&C, 1988).

Walter Houston Clark was born 15 July 02 in Westfield,
NJ, son of James Oliver and Eloise (Houston) Clark. He
attended Williams (B.A., 1925) and Harvard (A.M., 1926;
Ed.M., 1935; Ph.D., 1944). He was an instructor in
English and Bible, senior master and acting headmaster

at Lenox (MA) School (1926-45) and taught psychology at
Bowdoin (Brunswick, ME, 1945-7), psychology and
education at Middlebury (VT, 1947-51), and psychology
at Hartford (CT) Seminary Foundation in the School of
Religious Education (1951-62). He was Dean of the
School, 1952-62, and then taught psychology of religion
at Andover Newton Theological School (1962-67). He has
been a visiting professor at the University of Denver
((1948-49), Wesleyan (Middletown, CT, 1952-53), Tufts
(1967-68), and Furzedown (London, 1969). He was the
Finch Lecturer at Fuller (1971). He has been active in
professional groups: American Psychological
Association, American Association for the Advancement
of Science (Fellow), Society for the Scientific Study
of Religion (co-founder; pres, 1948-51; '64-66),
Religious Education Association, Academy of Religion
and Psychical Research (President, 1973). In addition
to numerous articles in education, psychology, religion
and the Encyclopaedia Britannica, he has published The
Oxford Group: Its History and Significance (NY:
Bookman, 1951), The Psychology of Religion: An
Introduction to Religious Experience and Behavior (NY:
Macmillan, 1958), Chemical Ecstasy: Psychedelic Drugs
and Religion (NY: Sheed & Ward, 1969), and with N.H.
Maloney, J. Daane and A.R. Tippett, Religious
Experience: Its Nature and Function in the Human Psyche
(Springfield, IL: Thomas, 1973). Several of these have
been translated into German and Swedish. On 24 July 30,
he married Ruth-Marie O'Brien. they have two children,
Walter Jr. and Jonathan. [See, Contemporary Authors,
37-40, p. 92].

Walter Harris claims his theological credentials are
highly suspect. Nevertheless, he is an avid fan of
analysis and synthesis and a devotee of great ideas and
great events. He possesses - somewhere (he says he is
not sure where he put it) - a Ph.D. from Syracuse
University. His field was human development and he
taught for several years at Pennsylvania State
University. Now he enjoys a career with the U.S.
Government in international communications. He raises
tomatoes and shovels snow in Brookfield, NH, pondering
the complex simplicity of nature, the rights of
individuals within a community, why most males but few
females enjoy making funny noises, the impossibility of
self-analysis, and Yin and Yang in all their
manifestations. Mr. Harris is 42 and describes himself
as often bemused.

Philip H. Hwang holds the B.A. in philosophy of religion from Seoul National University and his M.A. and Ph.D. from the University of Oklahoma (Norman) where he also taught for a time. His doctoral dissertation is a critical study of Mencius' "Philosophy of Human Nature with Special Reference to Kant and Confucius," available through University Microfilms in Ann Arbor, MI. He continues as Professor of Philosophy at Dongguk University - a Buddhist university - in Seoul. Among his several publications are an Introduction to the Philosophy of Religion, 3rd ed; Seoul: Chong Ro Publications, 1981. He was born into a Christian family and describes himself as a one-time Jesus freak. He has devoted his life to the comparative study of religion and philosophy, especially Confucianism, and to interfaith dialogue.

Theodore E. James earned the Doctorate in Philosophy from Columbia University, NYC. He is Professor Emeritus of Philosophy of Manhatten College, NYC, Lecturer at Fairfield University, adjunct professor of philosophy at St. Basil's Seminary in Stamford, CT, and St. Alphonsus Seminary in Suffield, CT. He has also taught at Sacred Heart University in Fairfield and at the Unification Theological Seminary. He is the author of Classics of Catholicism (NY: Philosophical Library, 19) and other scholarly works in philosophy.

The Venerable Sunanda Putuwar is the middle son of Kajibahadura and Dirghamaya Putuwar. He was born in Banepa, Nepal. A 1978 graduate of Mahamakut Buddhist University in Bangkok, Thailand, Putuwar also holds the MA (1981) from Banaras Hindu University (Varanasi, India), the MTS (1984) from Harvard and the Ph.D. (1988) in philosophy from American University's College of Arts and Sciences in Washington, D.C. Besides teaching in Thailand and his native Nepal, he has taught in several American schools and frequently interprets Buddhism to a wide variety of audiences. In Thailand, he became an ordained Theravada Buddhist monk and is currently a resident monk in Washington, D.C. Dr. Putuwar has authored a number of books and articles including, "Buddhist Marriage."

Yasar Nuri Ozturk was born in Bayburt on the Black Sea coast of Turkey, 1945. His ancestors came from Bagdad and include significant sheikhs of the Tasawwuf, the Sufi mystics of Islam. His father was a spiritual master of the Naqshibani order of Sufis. Yasar memorized the entire Quran as a child and learned both Persian and Arabic as well as being trained in Tasawwuf. After winning several literary contests, he moved to Istanbul and graduated from Istanbul University in Law and Theology. During this time he translated several works from Arabic to Turkish. He registered at the Istanbul Bar and became a practicing attorney. He left law after publishing his book on Mansur al-Hallaj and returned to the University for a doctorate in Islamic philosophy. He taught at the Faculty of Theology at Marmara University where he continues as Head of Sufi Studies. Among his many writings are works growing out of his studies of Muslim life in the Balkans, Germany, Switzerland, Saudi Arabia and Kuwait. His dozen books have been written in Turkish but several have been translated into English such as The Eye of the Heart and The Bektashi Order of Sufism.

Henry O. Thompson holds the B.Sc. (1953) from Iowa State, M.Div. (1958) and Ph.D. (1964) from Drew, M.Sc. in Education (1971) from Syracuse, M.A. in Educational Psychology (1975) and Diploma in School Psychology (1976) from Jersey City State and did graduate study at Rutgers in Newark (1978-80). He has taught at Upsala, Colgate-Rochester Divinity School, Syracuse, NY Theological Seminary, University of Jordan, Jersey City State, Unification Theological Seminary, Oberlin, Eastern and University of Pennsylvania. An ordained United Methodist, he has served churches in Minnesota and NJ. He worked as a pastoral counselor with the Institute for Personal and Family Relations and in archaeology (Shechem, 1960-68; Heshbon, 1968-73) with the American Center for Oriental Research (Director, 1971-2; Visiting Professor 72-3) in Amman. A US Air Force veteran (1st Lt), he is a member of the American Schools of Oriental Research, Archaeological Institute of America, Institute for Ultimate Reality and Meaning, Conference on Faith and History and others. He has authored, co-authored, edited and co-edited 20 books such as The Answers Lie Below, Put Your Future in Ruins, Biblical Archaeology, World Religions in War and Peace, Ethics in Nursing, etc. and several hundred articles, technical and popular.

Constantine N. Tsirpanlis is an historian, theologian and educator born in Kos, Greece, 18 Mar 35. He holds the Lic.Th., B.A., Halke Theological Seminary (1957), Th.M. from Harvard (1962), M.A. (1966) and Ph.D. (1970) from Columbia, Ph.D. from Fordham (1973) and Th.D. [ABD] from Union Theological Seminary (1966). He has been an instructor at NYU (1963-68), the New School of Social Research (modern Greek, 1968-70) and an adjunct professor at Mercy (1972), NY Institute of Technology (history, 1972-75), Delaware County Community College (1975-76), Dutchess Community College (1976-) and professor of church history and patristics at the Unification Theological Seminary (1975-). In 1981, he founded, and serves as president of, the American Institute of Patristics and Byzantine Studies, and is the founder of The Patristics and Byzantine Review. In addition to numerous articles, he has published A Short History of the Greek Language (1966), A Modern Greek Reader for American (1969), The Anthropology of St. John of Damascus (1967), A Modern Greek Idiom & Phrase Book (1978), Mark Eugenicus (1979), N. Cabasilas (1979), Greek Patristic Theology, vols. I-IV. He is a member of the American Society of Neohellenic Studies, Pan Dodecanisian Federation in the U.S., American Historical Association, American Philological Association, American Academy of Medieval Studies, International Association of Byzantine Studies, and the Hellenic Philological Association. On 12 July 75, he married Sophia Pappas and they have two children: Kalliope-Chrysoula and Nike.

Roger W. Wescott was born in Philadelphia in 1925. He holds the B.A. (summa cum laude, 1945) and Ph.D. in Linguistics (1948) from Princeton. He was a Rhodes Scholar at Oxford, did field work in Nigeria, founded and directed the African Language Program at Michigan State, became Professor of Linguistics (Graduate School) and of Anthropology (CLA) at Drew (1966) where he started the Department of Anthropology and chaired it for 12 years and became the Director of the Linguistics Program (1979-1988). He taught on the S.S. Universe of the University of Pittsburgh (1980), was Presidential Professor of Humanities and Social Science at the Colorado School of Mines (1980-81) is the first holder of The Endowed Chair of Excellence in the

Humanities at the University of Tennessee in Chattanooga (1988-89). Among 440 publications are 40 books such as The Divine Animal: An Exploration of Human Potentiality (NY: Funk & Wagnalls, 1969) and Sound and Sense: Linguistic Essays on Phonosemic Subjects (Jupiter, 1980). He serves as co-editor of Kronos, Futurics, and Forum Linguisticum and is past president of The Linguistic Association of Canada and the U.S. He is president - designate of the International Society for the Comparative Study of Civilizations (Mainz, Germany, and Urbana, IL). He is listed in Who's Who in the World, Who's Who in Educational Futuristics and The World's Who's Who of Authors. He has directed radio programs and appeared on network TV including hosting (1985, 1987) "Other Views." In 1982-83, he was a forensic linguist for NJ state courts.

INDEX

academic freedom
     writing and, v

agnostic
     position of, vii

antisemitism, 40

Aristotle, 64-70
     Metaphysics, 64, 65, 66-67
     practical wisdom, 69-71
     prudence (phronesis), 66, 69-71
     theoretical wisdom, 64-69
     truth, 65
     virtue, 65, 66
     wisdom, 63

atheist, vii

belief, 9-12 et passim
     Chinese, 51

biblical references, viii, 41, 44, 101-127
     I Corinthians, 73
     Ecclesiastes, vii-viii
     Ezekial, 47
     Luke, 73
     Matthew, vi
     Proverbs, 101
     Psalms, vi, vii
     Revelation, 47

biblical wisdom, 101-127
     Ancient Near East writings on, 105-106
     gift of God, 110, 111, 112
     Jeremiah and, 112
     quest for meaning in, 107-108, 111
     reflection on life and, 107
     Solomon and, 104-105, 111
     teachings on, 112-114
     tradition in, 101, 102-112, 115
     wisdom literature (The Writings), 101, 108, 123 fn.11
     wise men, 102, 103
     wise women, 103, 110

Buddhism

161

        training character, 53

faith
        definitions of, 71-72
        fear and, 74
        Holy Spirit and, 74
        hope of, 147
        in God, 51, 73
        reason and, 71-74
        religion and, vii
        science and, 73
        wisdom and, 63-78

free choice, 2-3

freedom, 3-7
        action,of, 2, 3, 10-11
        belief, of, 2, 9-12
        censorship and, 15
        choice, of, 2,3
        conflicts with, 2
        judgment and action in, 10-11
        privileges and, 11
        religion, of, 1-27
        rights and, 11
        speech, of, 2
        thought, of, 1, 2, 3, 9

freedom of information, 3, 6, 9

God (Lord, Supreme Being)
        Christianity and, 55
        creator, 109
        existence of, vii
        faith in, 51, 72
        fear of, 108
        foreign policy and, 44
        grace of, 59, 73-74
        heaven and, 53, 54
        language of, 111-112
        mysticism and, 80
        near death experiences with, 32
        personal, 51, 54, 57
        references to, 1
        Sufism and, 84, 85
        union with, 88
        wise, 63

humanism

traditions in, viii, ix
Sufism, 79-90

myth
    of eternal return, ix
    form of religious discourse, 147
    mythic tradition, ix
    nostalgia for past, 150, 151
    of paradise, 148

nationalism
    Christianity and, 36-48
    clergy and, 46
    definitions of, 36, 38
    fundamentalists and, 47
    national unity in, 38-39
    patriotic sacrifice for, 36, 40
    religion and, 35-50
    war and, 35, 40

near death experiences, 30-33
    descriptions of, 31, 32
    hell and, 32
    life after death beliefs, 32
    mysticism and, 30-34
    peace in, 31
    religious significance of, 32

Near East
    Ancient, vii, viii

New Testament teachings, 36, 47

peace
    clergy and, 48

persons
    free, 6
    language users, 4-7
    personhood and, 6
    prudent, 71
    wise (sophos), 63, 67-68, 70

philosophy
    as love of wisdom, 63, 101, 108
    logical reflection, xi
    natural, 68, 69
    of religion, xii

Dr. Matczak's, xii

sex, sexuality
      Christianity and, 12
      eroticism and, 15, 16
      humor and, 12, Figure 1, 13
      images and, fn. 26 p.22
      movies and, 15, 16
      respect for, 17

social liberation, 1

socio-logic(s), 1-27

spiritual beings
      in Confucianism, 52, 53, 56

spiritual liberation
      and religion, 1-2

Sufism
      action in, 84-86
      baga, 85, 86, 87
      definition of, 79, 82-84
      education of Sufi, 87
      fana, 85-86, 87
      farq, 87
      intellectual lineage in, 118
      jam, 87-88
      as mysticism, 79-90
      wisdom of Islam in, 79-90

teacher
      biblical, 112-114
      Confucius as, 53, fn. 8 p. 61
      as grandparents, 118
      as parents, 115-118
      wisdom in, 67

teaching
      art of, xi
      Confucius and, 53
      knowledge explosion and, 114-115

theism
      Christianity and, 55
      Confucianism and, 51-62

theology

DATE DUE